DIRECTIONS IN DEVELOPMENT

Labor Market Reform and Job Creation

The Unfinished Agenda in
Latin American and
Caribbean Countries

J. Luis Guasch

The World Bank
Washington, D.C.

J. Luis Guasch is lead economist for Latin America and the Caribbean Region and the Development Economics and Chief Economist Office at the World Bank, and Professor of Economics, University of California, San Diego. The author is grateful to Alejandra Cox-Edwards, Indermit Gill, James Heckman, Danny Leipziger, Constantino Lluch, Guillermo Perry, Carola Pessino,   Martin Rama, Joseph Stiglitz, and Lisa Taber for helpful comments; to Jorge Serraino and Joy Troncoso for technical support; and to Diane Stamm for editorial support.

Cover photograph, Netting Fish in Santa Marta, Colombia, by Edwin Huffman/World Bank. Cover design by Grammarians, Inc.

Library of Congress Cataloging-in-Publication Data

Guasch, J. Luis
    Labor market reform and job creation : the unfinished agenda in Latin
    American and Caribbean countries / J. Luis Guasch
        p.   cm.
    Includes bibliographical references.
    ISBN 0-8213-4415-3
        1. Labor market—Latin America.   2. Labor policy—Latin America.
    I. Title.
    HD5730.5.A6G8   1999
    331.12'042'09729—dc21
                                                                98-53590
                                                                CIP

Contents

List of Tables

List of Figures

List of Boxes

Foreword

Since 1990, most Latin American and Caribbean countries have undertaken significant structural reforms, liberalizing their economies through open trade regimes, privatizing state-owned enterprises, broadly deregulating their economies, and strengthening their financial sectors, and improving the impact of expenditures in the social sectors. Many of the results have been impressive: increased macroeconomic stability, resumption of growth (though, at least in many cases, not yet to the levels of earlier decades) and of significant capital flows (though, as we have recently seen, those flows have exposed the economy to enormous risks). Yet, despite that resumption of economic growth in most Latin American and Caribbean countries, improvements on the employment/unemployment front have been sluggish at best, with a few notable exceptions. After nearly a decade of moderate to high economic growth, the employment outlook in many countries remains worrisome. Persistent or increasing levels of unemployment, increasing shift in employment from the formal to the informal labor market, stagnant wages, and weak private-sector job creation performance, particularly in the formal sector, are raising serious social and economic concerns.

The main engine of *employment* growth is overall *economic* growth. But the relationship between employment growth and output growth, as this study illustrates, is greatly affected by the functioning, efficiency, and institutional structure of the labor market. For a given rate of economic growth, the induced employment growth largely depends on the characteristics of the labor market—and most importantly, its flexibility. Excessively protected labor markets and institutions that are riddled with distortions and rigidities weaken labor demand, hamper job creation, and make adjustments to the ever-changing structure of the economy more difficult, forcing the adjustments to take longer and to be more costly than would otherwise be the case. In some cases, the rigidities may even impede the adjustments entirely, thereby perpetuating inefficiencies. The deficiencies of the current structure of labor markets and institutions in Latin American countries have been exposed and enhanced by the stresses, the "shocks" induced by structural economic reforms.

This study examines the performance of labor markets in the Latin America and Caribbean region since 1990, the beginning (for most Latin American and Caribbean countries) of significant structural reforms. It shows the poor job creation performance, tracing that poor performance to the structure of labor markets, institutions, and incentives; it analyzes the effects of that structure on employment, earnings, income distribution and poverty levels, and labor demand. It also discusses the role of labor market institutions in labor market trends and the opportunities and options for reform. Such reforms have many dimensions, including changing taxes on labor, reducing the costs of labor force adjustments, and increasing contractual and wage flexibility to allow firms to compensate workers according to productivity and firm specific conditions, while protecting the essential rights of workers and providing for adequate safety nets. These types of reforms, as the evidence presented here strongly demonstrates, can favorably affect both employment growth and wage compensation.

This book was written to encourage a call for comprehensive labor market reforms—part of the unfinished agenda that is sometimes called the "second generation of reforms." These reforms are difficult: workers worry that their jobs may be put into jeopardy and, especially in economies where safety nets are inadequate, these concerns are real. Successful labor market reforms must thus be complemented with strengthening of the safety nets *and*—perhaps most importantly—with macroeconomic policies that sustain robust growth, particularly in the sectors that are likely to give rise to substantial job creation. The kinds of economic policies that some countries have pursued, especially in response to the financial crises of recent years, have led to economic contractions that contribute to a self-defeating and vicious cycle. Without growth, workers are unwilling to accept reforms that have a high risk of condemning them to extended periods of unemployment. But without the reforms, it is hard to generate high growth. Thus, meaningful work on the second generation of reforms—including reforms in the labor market—can only move forward aggressively in an economic climate in which governments commit themselves to sustained expansionary policies, and in which governments demonstrate a sensitivity to the real concerns of the working people. An ambitious agenda lies ahead, but the rewards of pursuing this agenda, with commitment and compassion, will be worth all the efforts devoted to it. We hope that the insights provided by this thoughtful and timely volume by Professor Guasch will provide both encouragement and understanding as countries embark upon these challenges upon which so much of their economic future depends.

Joseph Stiglitz
Chief Economist and
  Senior Vice President
The World Bank

Chapter 1
Introduction

Despite the resumption of economic growth in most Latin American and Caribbean (LAC) countries since the late 1980s, improvements on the employment/unemployment front have been sluggish at best, with a few notable exceptions.[1] In many countries, renewed growth in LAC in the 1990s has so far failed to generate adequate new jobs in place of those lost during the adjustment, and to restore wages to precrisis levels. After a number of years of relatively high economic growth, the employment outlook in many countries remains worrisome. In those countries where unemployment rates appear to be low, often as a result of how they are measured, the concern is the low quality and remuneration levels of available jobs. Persistent or increasing levels of unemployment, stagnant wages, and weak private sector job creation performance, particularly in the formal sector, are raising serious social and economic concerns.

First, because a larger share of the unemployed tend to be among the poorest 20 percent of the population, unemployment adversely affects poverty and income distribution. Second, long-term unemployment (duration), underemployment, and informality are also on the rise. Long-term unemployment is far more socially damaging than short-term, since those affected often become permanently separated from the labor force. Underemployment and informality are often linked to low earnings, at least for a significant share of informal workers, and to a lack of basic benefits, which worsen poverty and income distribution problems. Third, high levels of unemployment mean idleness of potentially productive workers and, thus, that output levels could be much higher. Finally, an environment where employment is perceived as a privilege unavailable to many, particularly the young, is bound to induce social tensions and breed sociopolitical instability. The recent patterns of unemployment increases, if persistent, may derail the significant economic reforms that have been realized since the late 1980s. If unemployment in LAC increases or persists at high levels, and the real gains associated with adjustment are not broadly shared, opposition to continued reforms is bound to increase.

To a large extent an initial employment shock induced by the structural economic reforms pursued by most countries in LAC was to be expected. These adjustments caused significant aggregate and sectoral labor displacement, particularly from the historically protected manufacturing sector and from parastatal companies (with their bloated employment levels). In Argentina, for example, the employment share of the manufacturing sec-

1

tor dropped from 25 percent in 1991 to about 20 percent in 1995, even while production was increasing. In Mexico that share dropped to 20.2 percent in 1995. Similarly, in Brazil in 1995 employment in the textile and apparel industries stood at around 500,000—roughly half its 1989 level, although production was 15 percent higher.

Increasing capital mobility, foreign trade, and the globalization of LAC economies means greater competition for firms. The opening of most LAC economies has reduced the cost of imports, helped to reduce inflation, and significantly reduced the cost of capital goods relative to the cost of labor (inducing an increase in the capital/labor ratio and, therefore, the productivity of labor), but has so far had significant costs in terms of labor displacement, which were expected to be short term.[2] Bloated employment levels prior to the reforms, coupled with the technological innovations and technical progress adopted in response to competitive pressures, have induced substantial shifts in demand away from unskilled workers toward skilled workers.[3] The increase in demand for skilled workers in LAC has far outweighed supply shifts and has raised their wages, widening in many countries the earnings gap between skilled and unskilled labor.[4] Large investment and the accompanying substitution of labor for capital appears to be correlated with increased wage inequality. The decrease in demand for unskilled workers and for skilled workers with obsolete or inappropriate skills has induced increased unemployment in many LAC countries. All these elements have led to wide corporate restructuring and a surplus of unskilled labor, which often translates into higher unemployment, higher informality, lower tax revenue from employment taxes, and greater pressure on state resources—particularly under rigid labor markets—and to increased claims for government intervention for job creation and training.[5]

Compounding the employment problem, high rates of labor force growth and the steady increase in labor force participation have combined with slack private-sector job creation to produce increasingly informal employment and open unemployment growth in many LAC economies. At the same time, disparities remain or are increasing with regard to the wage gap between skilled and unskilled labor and the number and type of jobs being created, as well as their distribution among households at various income levels.

In a number of countries where economic reforms have produced a low inflation environment in the mid- to late-1990s, embedded wage rigidities have favored employment adjustments over wage adjustments. While job destruction was expected from these reforms, so was job creation. However, the latter has been slow to develop and lags considerably behind medium-term expectations. In short, current rates of economic growth are generating fewer jobs than are needed to absorb the growing labor force in a productive way. This situation was initially interpreted as a specific consequence of the early stages of the reform process, but it now appears to have become permanent, even in cases where the reform process is at an advanced stage and growth rates are relatively high.

While undoubtedly the main engine of employment growth is economic growth, the relationship is greatly affected by the labor market's functioning, efficiency, and institutional structure. For a given rate of economic growth, the induced employment growth largely depends on the flexibility of the labor market.[6] This is best illustrated by the striking differential employment growth performance in the last two decades between the United States and European countries. While both have enjoyed similar economic growth rates, the former, with a very flexible labor market, has produced strong yearly employment growth of around 2 to 3 percent, while the latter, with rigid labor markets and significant welfare benefits, have had negative or no employment growth.

Moreover, the demand for labor in response to lower labor costs is usually twice the response to increases in GDP (gross domestic product) growth. The labor demand response to increases in GDP is also favorably affected, in terms of size and speed, by increases in the flexibility of labor markets. Thus, labor reforms exert a powerful impact on employment, coupled with resumed sustainable GDP growth. These are the arguments and the case for labor reforms.

To a large extent, for any given economic growth rate, the relatively poor job-creation response and performance in many LAC economies can be attributed to a lack of factors markets reform—particularly in the labor market and in the early stages of the liberalization process. In most LAC countries, labor markets continue to be highly regulated, relying on labor laws enacted in the 1950s and 1960s that favor significant employment protection in the private sector and lifelong job security in the public sector, and that heavily tax labor and adjustments in the firms' labor force. Additional rigidities appear in the area of wage determination, with most collective bargaining contracts highly centralized, establishing fixed bimonthly or monthly wages and making little use of bonuses linked to performance. Protected labor markets and institutions that are riddled with distortions and rigidities weaken labor demand in itself, and, in response to GDP growth, make adjustment to the new (efficient) equilibrium longer and more socially costly or, worse yet, in some economies induce a new, inefficient equilibrium. While there is significant variance across countries, the institutional structure of most LAC countries is not friendly to job creation and in the current low inflation environment tends to induce responses to shocks through employment adjustments rather than wage adjustments. Past education investment policies favoring tertiary education and neglecting the quality, delivery, and coverage of primary and secondary education are also factors, since the consequences are a relatively uneducated and untrained labor force and a mismatch between demanded and supplied skills.

The deficiencies of the current structure of labor markets and institutions in LAC countries have been exposed and enhanced by the shocks induced by structural economic reforms. If the price of labor does not adjust quickly and smoothly to macroeconomic shocks or to secular changes in the macroeconomic environment, then either the quantity of labor must adjust or the rates of output growth or inflation are likely to do so. When fluctuations in aggregate demand occur, changes in the employment level tend to be much smaller in economies with flexible labor markets, such as the United States or East Asian countries, than in other regions such as Latin America and the Caribbean. The former economies usually adjust to downturns through wage changes without laying off significant numbers of workers, or if there are layoffs, they are often temporary, with unemployment duration relatively low. With increased globalization and its associated competitive pressures and low inflation environments, a continued high degree of labor protection by the state seems unsustainable and to some extent contradictory, since countries with higher labor costs reduce their competitiveness. Yet very few countries in the Latin American and Caribbean region have engaged in comprehensive labor reforms, which have proven to be politically difficult; only Chile and Colombia have done this in the liberalization process's earlier stages. Peru did it in the medium stages. Chile, Colombia, and Peru have been leading the region in major labor market reforms that increase overall labor market flexibility. These reforms have proven to be effective in facilitating job creation and decreasing unemployment, adjusted for the economic cycle. A few other countries have engaged in some partial reforms, but they do not seem to circumscribe a pattern for overall flexibility. Others, like Argentina, Brazil, and Nicaragua, are in the process of passing wide-ranging labor market reforms.

The persistence of high rates of unemployment, weak private-sector job creation rates, stagnant wage growth, and an ever-increasing informal sector in moderate-to-high GDP growth economies, with their accompanying social and economic implications, are generating new calls for reforms and debate about the most appropriate policies to deal with these critical problems. Above all, the objective of labor market reforms is *not* to lower wages, but to eliminate inefficiencies and waste, reduce transaction costs, better align costs and benefits of labor taxes, and introduce contractual and wage flexibility allowing firms to compensate according to productivity and firm-specific conditions while providing a fair and adequate safety net for unemployed workers. In the process, distributional impacts might occur, such as a lower rate of wage growth for the protected sector and increased wage dispersion, but overall welfare will increase. These reforms will favorably affect both employment growth and wage compensation.

This book focuses on (a) the performance of labor markets in the Latin American and Caribbean region since the beginning of the significant structural reforms most countries in the region have undertaken; (b) the structure of labor markets, institutions, and incentive structures; (c) the effects of that structure on employment, earnings, income distribution, and poverty levels; (d) the role of labor market institutions in labor market trends; (e) the options for reform and the benefits of comprehensive labor reforms, as evidenced inside and outside the region; and (f) labor policy reforms to improve in a sustainable way the employment/unemployment outlook.

Chapter 2
Unemployment Performance in Latin American and Caribbean Countries during 1990–98

Persistence of Unemployment

Open unemployment remains persistent and has actually been increasing in a number of LAC countries since 1990, as shown in tables 2.1 and 2.2, although compared to the 1985 level it has improved. While considerable variation exists across countries, with some showing significant improvements, open unemployment for Latin America as a whole has increased from 5.7 percent in 1990 to 8.5 percent in 1998. The ILO estimate for 1999 is 9.5 percent—although it will likely be higher, since the estimate predates the January 1999 sharp devaluation of the Brazilian real, which will negatively affect economic growth in LAC countries. A few country examples illustrate the predicament.

In Brazil, open unemployment has recently increased—reaching 9.3 percent as of January 1999—as a result of restraints imposed on the economy to avoid overheating and as a response to the 1997 East Asia financial crisis. Despite a cumulative GDP increase of nearly 15 percent during 1993–95, the number of jobs created was insufficient to absorb the labor force, and open urban unemployment increased from 4.8 percent to nearly 6 percent countrywide over the period, reaching 16 percent in greater Sao Paulo in 1996. Since the late 1980s, the proportion of regularly employed urban workers has fallen to less than one-half of the work force, with the rest joining the ever-growing informal economy or the ranks of the self-employed (mostly in the service sector).

Due partly to the 1995 recession, Mexico's open urban unemployment rate climbed in 1996 to 5.8 percent, or more than double its early 1990s rate. Strong economic growth in 1997 and 1998, and flexible real wages (a drop of more than 20 percent since 1994) reduced that rate to 3.3 percent in 1998 (World Bank 1998). Argentina, despite an impressive average GDP growth of 8.9 percent per year during 1990–94, saw its unemployment rate climb from 6.5 percent in 1991 to an unprecedented peak of 17.5 percent in 1995.[7] In Montevideo, Uruguay, open unemployment rose from 8.6 percent in 1989 to 12.2 percent in 1997. The Caribbean countries, with about half the labor force growth rates of the Latin American countries, have among the highest unemployment rates in the region, stubbornly anchored near 16 percent. Bolivia, Chile, Ecuador, Guatemala, Honduras, and Peru achieved improvements in their unemployment rates, although progress in a number of these countries has been inconsistent, with Chile being the exception.

Not only has unemployment been increasing in a number of countries throughout the region, but the tendency has been toward an increase in duration of unemployment. In Argentina, for example, the mean duration of a completed unemployment spell went from 13 weeks in 1991 to 45 weeks in 1995. Similar trends are observed in Uruguay, Venezuela, Brazil, and Caribbean countries.

Incidence of Unemployment

Not surprisingly, across the region the unemployment rate in the first poorest decile is four or more times higher than the average unemployment rate. The rate for the poorest 20 percent of households is three or more times the average. These ratios do not appear to be affected much by fluctuations in overall unemployment. In addition, unemployment for the period was higher among women, youths, and the uneducated. Throughout LAC, women's unemployment rate exceeded the average by between 10 and 40 percent, while the unemployment rate of persons aged 20 to 24 exceeded the average by more than 50 percent. For persons aged 15 to 24, the unemployment rate was twice the average rate.

A caveat is in order about the unemployment numbers. Because of the unemployment measurement methodology, numbers cited should be considered to underestimate the real unemployment levels. In measuring unemployment, most Latin American countries follow the International Labor Organization (ILO) recommendation that the employed population should consist of those who had worked at least one hour in the week before they were surveyed. Those who did not work but were certain to return to a job or business, and those who were going to begin a new job in the next four weeks, are also included. The open unemployed are those who did not work but were available to engage in some economic activity and sought to do so in the two months prior to the survey. While this definition is also used in OECD countries, it makes more sense for them; their numbers are hardly comparable to those of developing countries. In most OECD countries little economic informality exists, and the split between employed and unemployed is sharper. Those employed are mostly full-time workers. In developing countries, to some extent as a result of limited or nonexistent unemployment benefits, many so-called employed workers are really informal workers who work a few hours a week for very low remuneration.

Table 2.1 Latin America and the Caribbean, Urban Open Unemployment, 1985-98

	1985	1986	1987	1988	1989	1990	1991	1992	1993	1994	1995	1996	1997	1998
Latin America														
Argentina	6.1	5.6	5.9	6.3	7.8	7.5	6.5	7.0	9.6	11.5	17.5	17.3	14.9	13.2
Bolivia	5.7	7.0	5.7	11.5	9.5	7.2	5.9	5.4	5.9	3.0	3.6	4.0	4.4	4.7
Brazil	5.3	3.6	3.7	3.8	3.3	4.3	4.8	4.9	5.4	5.1	4.6[d]	5.4	7.0	9.3
Colombia	13.8	13.5	11.8	11.3	9.9	10.5	10.2	10.2	8.6	8.9	8.8	11.3	12.4	15.1
Costa Rica	6.7	6.7	5.9	6.3	3.7	5.4	6.0	4.3	4.0	4.3	5.7	6.6	5.9	6.2
Chile	17.0	13.1	11.9	10.0	7.2	6.4	7.1	4.9	4.1	6.3	6.6	6.8	6.6	6.8
Dominican Rep.	—	—	—	—	—	—	19.6	20.3	19.9	16.0	15.8	16.5	15.9	16.5
Ecuador	10.4	10.7	7.2	7.4	7.9	6.1	8.5	8.9	8.3	7.1	6.9	10.4	9.3	10.3
El Salvador	—	—	—	9.4	8.4	10.0	7.5	6.8	—	7.0[a]	7.0	5.8	7.5	—
Guatemala	12.0	14.0	11.4	8.8	6.2	6.3	6.7	6.1	8.1	7.2	—	—	—	—
Honduras	11.7	12.1	11.4	8.7	7.2	6.9	7.1	5.1	5.6	4.0	6.6	6.6	5.2	6.3
Mexico	4.4	4.3	3.9	3.5	2.9	2.8	2.7	2.8	3.4	3.6	6.3	5.5	4.1	3.3
Panama	15.7	12.7	14.1	21.1	20.4	20.0	20.0	18.2	15.6	15.8	16.9	16.9	15.4	15.8
Paraguay	5.1	6.1	5.5	4.7	6.1	6.6	5.1	5.3	5.1	4.1	5.5	8.2	7.1	7.4
Peru	10.1	5.3	4.8	7.1	7.9	8.3	5.9	9.4	9.9	8.8	7.9	8.1	8.4	8.0
Uruguay	13.1	10.7	9.3	9.1	8.6	9.2	8.9	9.0	8.4	9.2	10.8	12.4	12.2	10.2
Venezuela	14.3	12.1	9.9	7.9	9.7	11.0	10.1	8.0	6.9	9.0	10.9	12.3	11.9	11.3
Latin America	10.1[a]	—	—	—	—	8.2	8.4	8.1	8.1	7.8	8.8	9.3	10.0	10.3[d]
	8.3[b]	—	—	—	—	5.7	5.6	5.7	6.1	6.3	7.2	7.7	7.6	8.5[d]

The Caribbean^c

Barbados	18.7	17.8	17.9	17.5	14.7	15.0	17.3	23.0	24.3	21.9	19.7	14.5	19.5	12.7
Jamaica	25.0	23.7	21.0	18.9	18.0	15.3	15.7	15.7	16.3	15.4	16.2	16.0	16.0	15.6
T. and Tobago	15.7	17.2	22.2	22.0	22.0	20.0	18.5	19.6	19.8	18.4	17.2	16.2	15.0	14.0

Note:
a. Arithmetic average.
b. Weighted average.
c. Not included in the average since the methodology used in the Caribbean countries differs from the one used in Latin America.
d. Averages only include countries for which 1998 information was available.
— denotes data not available.
Source: ILO and World Bank.

Table 2.2 Open Unemployment Rate in Main Latin American Cities, 1990–98 (Percentage)

	1990	1991	1992	1993	1994	1995	1996	1997	1998
Argentina	7.5	6.5	7.0	9.6	11.5	17.5	17.3	14.9	13.2
G.B.Aires	7.3	5.8	6.7	10.1	12.1	18.8	18.4	15.7	14.1
Córdoba	5.8	4.8	5.1	6.8	8.7	15.5	17.2	17.4	12.7
G.Mendoza	5.9	4.3	4.3	4.5	5.6	6.8	7.0	7.0	7.0
G.Rosario	8.5	10.2	9.3	11.3	12.8	19.7	19.0	14.7	11.7
G. Tucumán	10.5	11.6	12.3	13.0	14.5	19.6	20.2	15.8	14.8
Bolivia	7.2	5.9	5.5	5.9	3.1	3.6	4.0	4.4	4.7
La Paz	7.1	6.6	7.4	5.6	3.2	4.2	4.4	5.4	5.6
Brasil	4.3	4.8	4.9	5.4	5.1	4.6	5.4	7.0	9.3
R.Janeiro	3.5	3.6	3.4	4.1	4.1	3.4	3.8	3.8	5.5
Sao Paulo	4.6	5.5	5.4	5.8	5.4	5.2	6.7	8.0	8.8
B.Horizonte	4.1	4.1	4.1	4.5	4.2	3.8	5.2	5.2	7.1
P.Alegre	3.7	4.4	4.0	4.1	4.1	4.4	5.8	5.8	7.8
Salvador	5.4	5.7	5.6	6.6	7.0	6.8	8.0	8.0	9.6
Recife	5.7	5.9	7.1	8.9	6.8	5.6	6.1	6.1	9.6
Chile	7.4	7.1	6.2	6.4	7.8	6.6	5.4	6.6	6.8
Colombia	10.5	10.2	10.2	8.6	8.9	8.8	11.3	12.4	15.1
Barranquilla	10.9	9.7	10.9	10.0	10.5	11.0	11.7	12.4	11.6
Bogotá	9.4	8.6	8.3	6.5	7.1	9.3	10.1	11.7	13.5
Cali	9.6	9.4	9.6	9.2	9.9	14.1	17.3	10.1	20.6
Medellín	12.5	13.8	13.8	11.9	10.5	12.6	14.5	17.3	16.0
Costa Rica	5.4	6.0	4.3	4.0	4.3	5.7	6.6	5.9	6.2
Ecuador	6.1	8.5	8.9	8.3	7.1	6.9	10.4	9.3	10.3
México	2.8	2.7	2.8	3.4	3.6	6.3	5.5	4.1	3.3
C.de México	3.3	3.0	3.4	4.0	4.1	6.3	4.5	4.5	3.8
Guadalajara	1.7	2.5	3.1	3.0	3.4	5.3	3.3	3.3	2.7
Monterrey	3.6	3.5	3.2	4.8	5.1	5.9	3.9	3.9	3.3
Panamá	—	—	—	—	—	—	—	—	—
Panamá A.M.	20.0	20.0	18.2	15.6	15.8	16.4	16.9	15.4	15.8
Paraguay	7.5	10.4	14.4	—	4.4	5.2	8.2	7.1	7.4
Asunción	6.6	5.1	5.3	5.1	4.1	5.5	9.2	6.4	7.0
Perú	—	—	—	—	—	8.5	7.9	8.4	8.0
Lima									
Metropolitana	8.3	5.9	9.4	9.9	8.8	7.9	7.9	9.2	8.4
Uruguay	8.5	8.9	9.0	8.3	9.2	10.3	11.9	11.5	10.2
Montevideo	9.2	8.9	9.0	8.4	9.2	10.8	12.4	11.6	10.7
Venezuela	11.0	10.1	8.1	6.8	8.9	10.9	12.3	11.9	11.3

Source: ILO and household surveys, and World Bank

Chapter 3
Employment Performance: Continued Mismatch between Employment Growth and Labor Force Growth

Insufficient Employment Growth

Employment Growth
While for most countries the rate of growth of employment has been positive and significant by many standards, it has not often been large enough to absorb the growing labor force in many Latin American and Caribbean countries, as shown in table 3.1. The comparison between labor force and employment growth (both formal and informal) throughout the region illustrates the severity of this situation. While the average annual employment growth rate in LAC during 1990–97 was 2.9 percent, the average annual labor force growth rate was 3.2 percent. In 1998 employment growth was 2.6 percent while the labor force increased by 3.2 percent. In 1995, a crisis year in many LAC countries as a result of Mexican devaluation, employment grew by only 2 percent, while the labor force climbed by 3.2 percent. The trend is clear: employment is growing more slowly than the labor force by a widening margin. (See figure 3.1 for the example of Argentina.) The result is a combination of ever-higher unemployment and/or informality (underemployment).

Continued Increases in Labor Force Participation
The rate of demographic growth, while still high, has slowed in the 1990s. However, it is the children born during the population boom of the 1970s and the early 1980s who are now entering the work force, and placing added strain on the employment/unemployment outlook (see table 3.2). Moreover, the number of net jobs needed to absorb the new workers is larger than the rates shown here, since labor force participation is on the increase in LAC. By 1998, labor force participation had increased by 3 percent on average over the 1995 figures. For example, the working-age population in Ecuador grew during 1982–93 by 2.7 percent annually, on average, while labor force participation increased at an annual rate of 4.6 percent; total labor force participation jumped from 43 percent in 1982 to more than 50 percent in 1990. Labor force participation is rising, particularly among women.

Figure 3.1 Labor Force and Employment Growth in Argentina, 1980–95

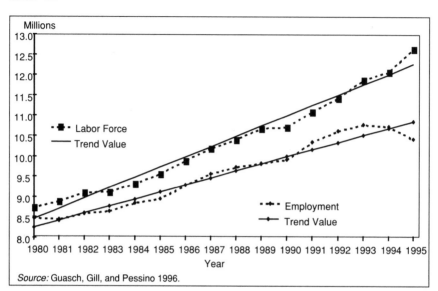

Source: Guasch, Gill, and Pessino 1996.

During the last 10 years the labor force participation rate for females in many LAC countries has increased by between 5 and 10 percentage points. Further, since these rates are still relatively low—in the 30 to 50 percent range—still more increases can be expected, again adversely affecting the employment–unemployment picture.

In Ecuador the participation of women in the labor market increased from 34 percent in 1988 to 46 percent in 1993. In Argentina, female labor force participation in the greater Buenos Aires area increased from 43 percent in 1987 to 49 percent in 1994. In Colombia, where one female in three was working in 1976, one in two was working in 1996.

Aside from the expected trend increases in labor force participation due to demographics, reduced fertility, and increased schooling of women, cyclical factors are also behind the recent increases in labor force participation rates. Changes in labor force participation rates can be attributed to two factors: (a) an *income effect*—that is, change in work force participation due to a change in family income, and (b) a *substitution effect*—that is, the change in participation due to a change in the price of labor. These are also referred to, respectively, as the "added worker" and the "drop-out" (or "discouraged worker") effects in this report. A decline in household income that occurs because the family head has become unemployed, for instance, may lead to other members (for example, spouse, school-aged children) entering the labor force, thus resulting in more workers. Similarly, a fall in workers' wages may lead them to drop out of the labor force entirely because they do not perceive the wages they would earn as worth the effort expended. That is, workers prefer "leisure" to working at the prevailing wage rate.

Table 3.1 Annual Growth Rates, 1990–97 and 1998

				Productivity	
Countries	GDP	EAP	Employment	1990–97	1998
Argentina	5.5	3.0	1.8	3.6	0.1
Barbados	0.8	1.5	1.4	–0.6	0.1
Bolivia	2.8	2.7	2.5	0.3	–0.2
Brazil	3.9	3.2	3.7	0.2	—
Chile	7.1	3.2	3.5	3.4	3.5
Colombia	4.1	3.3	3.0	1.0	1.0
Costa Rica	3.4	3.9	3.8	–0.4	—
Ecuador	3.5	4.5	4.0	–0.5	—
Honduras	3.7	4.8	4.9	–1.1	—
Jamaica	0.5	1.2	1.0	–0.5	–1.6
Mexico	2.8	3.9	3.7	–0.9	–0.9
Panama	4.8	5.4	6.3	–1.4	0.0
Paraguay	2.7	5.6	5.6	–2.7	—
Peru	5.5	3.5	3.2	2.2	–1.4
Dom. Republic	4.7	1.2	2.7	1.9	—
Trinidad & Tobago	1.9	2.1	3.0	–1.1	0.6
Uruguay	4.2	1.9	1.4	2.8	–0.7
Venezuela	2.9	3.1	2.6	0.3	–6.0
Latin America and the Caribbean	3.5	3.1	2.9	0.6	0.0

			1998		
	GDP	EAP	Employment	Productivity	
Latin America and the Caribbean	2.6	3.2	2.6	0.0	

Note: EAP = economically active population.
Source: ILO.

Table 3.2 Labor Force Participation Rates

Countries	Total[a] 1970	1980	1985	1990	1995	Male[a] 1970	1980	1985	1990	1995	Female[a] 1970	1980	1985	1990	1995
Argentina	49.2	47.1	49.0	50.5	51.4	73.9	71.1	69.0	66.5	66.9	24.5	24.1	29.9	35.3	36.7
Barbados	50.3	58.7	60.5			65.1	66.0	68.4			36.7	52.3	55.4		
Bolivia	46.5	46.9	47.0	48.9	50.1	74.6	71.4	69.0	68.1	67.8	19.5	23.4	26.0	30.5	32.9
Brazil	44.9	55.0	55.9	56.3	56.8	71.5	76.1	76.3	76.1	75.3	18.4	34.0	35.5	36.7	38.5
Chile	41.2	41.3	43.2	44.9	47.0	65.4	63.0	64.2	65.1	66.0	18.1	20.4	23.0	25.4	28.7
Colombia	44.5	45.3	46.8	48.7	50.3	69.6	64.8	64.5	65.7	66.4	20.2	26.2	29.6	32.4	34.7
Costa Rica	44.9	46.2	47.6	48.8	49.9	72.9	728.0	74.0	73.7	73.3	16.7	19.3	20.8	23.6	26.2
Cuba	41.9	44.0	46.4	50.8	53.8	67.0	61.0	62.8	67.3	70.1	15.9	26.7	29.8	34.2	37.4
Ecuador	44.1	43.1	45.3	47.6	49.4	74.2	69.3	69.0	70.7	71.1	14.0	16.9	20.7	24.4	27.6
El Salvador	49.8	47.4	46.1	45.2	47.3	78.6	73.4	70.2	67.8	68.6	20.9	22.7	23.3	24.3	27.5
Guatemala	44.6	42.2	43.3	44.4	45.7	76.6	71.3	71.0	70.5	70.5	11.8	12.6	15.3	17.9	20.7
Guyana	42.3	45.9	47.5			67.9	70.3	71.8			17.1	22.3	23.6		
Haiti	72.7	62.7	58.3	58.8	59.0	80.4	73.6	70.8	70.6	70.3	65.5	52.6	46.7	47.6	48.4
Honduras	45.4	46.2	48.2	50.0	51.1	78.6	76.7	77.0	78.9	77.8	12.3	15.7	18.4	21.0	24.3
Jamaica	57.3	59.3	62.3			68.6	65.8	68.7			46.9	53.1	56.0		
Mexico	40.4	47.8	47.9	48.9	51.1	65.7	71.3	70.7	71.3	72.4	15.2	24.6	25.7	27.1	30.5
Nicaragua	43.5	48.8	51.2	51.5	52.3	69.9	70.6	70.8	70.2	69.7	17.7	27.4	32.0	33.3	35.3
Panama	50.3	44.0	45.5	47.4	49.4	73.7	63.1	64.6	66.5	67.6	26.0	24.2	25.9	28.0	31.0
Paraguay	46.5	47.6	48.3	49.2	49.3	73.9	76.5	76.1	74.2	73.0	19.6	18.9	20.6	24.0	25.3
Peru	46.9	48.7	60.0	51.0	52.3	67.6	67.7	68.4	68.7	69.3	26.0	29.5	31.6	33.5	35.7
Dominican Rep.	50.2	50.6	52.5	54.4	56.1	75.0	73.6	74.5	75.5	76.2	24.0	26.8	29.7	32.6	35.3
Suriname	40.2	39.4	41.2			60.7	57.7	59.3			20.0	21.6	23.6		
T. & Tobago	46.5	47.1	49.1			66.8	68.7	69.5			27.0	27.0	26.8		
Uruguay	48.5	49.2	52.2	52.6	53.4	71.4	66.9	67.0	66.7	67.4	26.2	32.4	38.3	39.5	40.3
Venezuela	41.7	44.4	46.5	48.1	49.6	65.2	66.3	67.4	67.7	67.9	17.8	22.0	25.3	28.2	31.2

Note: a. Economically active population aged 10 years and over as percentage of the total population aged 10 years and over.
Source: ILO.

For any particular group of workers (for example, classified by age or sex), the only way to distinguish between the two effects is if (a) income and substitution effects differ significantly among households and/or (b) the relationship between the real income of primary workers and the real wages of secondary workers has moved differently for different types of households. In most of these studies, labor force participation rates are postulated to be functions of a time trend (to capture long-term social trends not otherwise captured in the analysis) and a cyclical factor (to capture short-term fluctuations in economic activity). If labor force participation moves in the opposite direction from economic activity (that is, it goes up as economic activity goes down), this indicates the "added worker" effect predominates. If, in contrast, both labor force participation and economic activity go down, that indicates the "discouraged worker" effect dominates. The main measure used as an indicator of cyclical activity is the unemployment rate of prime-aged men. The evidence in a number of LAC countries is the predominance of the "added worker" effect or the countercyclical quality of labor force participation (World Bank 1997a). An increase in the incidence of unemployment among heads of households has pushed more of households' secondary workers (spouses and children) into the labor force, worsening the unemployment outlook.

Deficient "Good" Employment Growth

Increased Underemployment

The real unemployment rate is actually higher than the figures reported above, since a number of LAC countries have increasingly tended to substitute full-time jobs for informal and part-time jobs. For example, in Mexico, while the unemployment rate in 1994 was 3.6 percent, if workers who involuntarily worked less than 15 hours a week were included, the rate climbed to 5 percent; including those who involuntarily work less than 35 hours a week, the unemployment rate climbed to 25.5 percent. The figures are similar for other countries. In Argentina, the employment share of part-time workers counted as employed increased from 8 percent in 1990 to nearly 14 percent in 1998, and part-time jobs increased from 12 to 16 percent of total employment. According to government figures, the national *underemployment* rate is estimated to be 75 percent in Peru and 55 percent in Nicaragua. The underemployed are often either independent own-account (self-employed) workers, or flexibly linked to the formal sector as casual, temporary, and home-based workers. These jobs tend to be low income, provide little or no benefits, and on average have an adverse impact on poverty and income distribution.

Increasing Informal Sector Share of Employment

Significant numbers of informal sector workers are counted as employed in the statistics, though their employment situation may be quite tenuous. According to ILO numbers, 59 percent of the region's workers were employed in the informal sector in 1998, compared to 51.6 percent in 1990. The informal sector has, in fact, been the main source of job creation in LAC. The ILO estimates that during 1990–98, 88 out of each 100 new jobs created corresponded to the informal sector; of the estimated 15.7 million new jobs created in Latin America and the Caribbean, 13.6 million were in the informal sector. Microenterprises were the main generators of employment, where new jobs increased by 5.5 percent annually during 1990–95, and by 4.5 percent in 1998.

Medium and large private firms' share of the employment sector has decreased in all countries except Argentina, Ecuador, Honduras, Panama, and Uruguay, as shown in table 3.3. Employment in the formal sector has been growing at a meager 1 percent per year. According to ILO data, every Latin American country experienced an increase in the proportion of informal sector employment during 1990–96. In Ecuador, the informal sector share rose from 45 percent of total employment in 1990 to 48 percent in 1993, (with 80 percent informality in commerce); in Peru, the informal sector employment share increased from 51.8 percent of total employment in 1990 to 58 percent in 1996; in Mexico it went from 56 to 60 percent, and in Venezuela, from 39 to 48 percent. In 1996, 27.2 percent of the workers in the region as a whole were self-employed, with 7.1 percent engaged in domestic service and 23.1 percent employed in establishments with fewer than 10 workers. Of those employed, 42.6 percent were engaged in the formal sector, 13 percent were employed in the public sector, and the remaining 29.6 percent worked in private firms. Even using a more restrictive definition of the informal sector than the ILO's, (including self-employed workers other than professionals and administrative workers), the same pattern emerges, with increases in the share of informal sector workers among the employed. (Appendix 1 presents an analysis of informality in Mexico.)

Selective Improvements

Some countries, including Bolivia, Chile, and Peru, have shown sustained improvements on the employment–unemployment front. In common, they have relatively high GDP growth rates and greater labor market flexibility attributable to labor market and institutional reforms. Other countries, like Colombia, Guatemala, Honduras, Mexico, and Paraguay, have shown overall employment improvements (although they have worsened in 1995–96, except for Mexico) despite moderate or low GDP growth rates. Not surprisingly, a positive correlation exists between the region's employment and GDP growth. Finally, the service sector, as expected, has been the major provider of new jobs and employment growth, although many of those are at the lower end of the wage spectrum. This sector now accounts for 50 to 70 percent of the region's total employment, yet it is often the poorest in terms of information and data, as opposed to the manufacturing sector, which accounts for only 20 to 30 percent of total employment and is declining.

Table 3.3 Latin America: Nonagricultural Employment Structure (Percentage)

| Country /Year | Total | Informal Sector | | | Formal Sector | | |
		Self-Employed[a]	Domestic Service	Small Business[b]	Total	Public Sector	Medium and Large Private Firms
Latin America							
1990	51.6	24.7	6.7	20.2	48.4	15.3	33.0
1991	52.4	25.0	6.7	20.7	47.6	15.2	32.5
1992	53.0	25.6	6.7	20.8	47.0	14.6	32.3
1993	53.9	25.3	7.1	21.6	46.1	13.7	32.4
1994	54.9	25.8	7.0	22.1	45.1	13.3	31.8
1995	56.1	26.5	7.1	22.5	43.9	13.2	30.8
1996	57.4	27.2	7.1	23.1	42.6	13.0	29.6
1997	57.7	27.1	7.6	23.0	42.3	13.0	29.3
Argentina							
1990	47.5	24.7	7.9	14.9	52.5	19.3	33.2
1991	48.6	25.3	7.9	15.4	51.4	18.5	32.9
1992	49.6	25.9	7.8	15.9	50.4	17.7	32.7
1993	50.8	26.6	7.9	16.3	49.2	16.8	32.4
1994	52.5	27.0	7.4	18.1	47.5	14.3	33.2
1995	53.3	27.2	7.6	18.5	46.7	13.8	32.9
1996	53.6	27.1	7.8	18.7	46.4	13.2	33.2
1997	53.8	26.5	8.1	19.2	46.2	12.7	33.5
Bolivia							
1990	56.9	37.7	6.4	12.8	43.1	16.5	26.6
1991	56.1	37.8	6.8	11.5	43.9	17.1	26.8
1992	56.6	38.2	5.9	12.5	43.4	15.5	27.9
1993	61.2	36.4	6.5	18.3	38.8	12.7	26.1
1994	61.3	37.1	5.2	19.0	38.7	11.4	27.3
1995	63.6	39.6	5.4	18.6	36.4	11.4	25.0
1996	63.1	37.7	5.5	19.9	36.9	11.1	25.9
1997	56.6	35.4	4.0	17.2	43.4	11.1	32.3

(Table continues on the following page.)

Table 3.3 (continued)

Country /Year	Informal Sector				Formal Sector		
	Total	Self-Employed[a]	Domestic Service	Small Business[b]	Total	Public Sector	Medium and Large Private Firms
Brazil							
1990	52.0	21.0	7.7	23.3	48.0	11.0	36.9
1991	53.2	21.7	7.7	23.8	46.8	10.7	36.1
1992	54.3	22.5	7.8	24.0	45.7	10.4	35.2
1993	56.5	21.9	8.9	24.7	44.5	9.7	34.8
1994	58.4	22.4	9.2	25.0	43.5	9.7	33.8
1995	57.6	23.0	9.4	25.2	42.4	9.6	32.8
1996	59.3	23.8	9.5	26.0	40.7	9.6	31.1
1997	60.4	24.3	9.8	26.3	39.6	9.3	30.3
Colombia							
1990	55.2	23.5	5.4	26.3	44.8	9.6	35.2
1991	55.7	23.7	5.3	26.7	44.3	9.3	35.0
1992	55.8	23.7	5.2	27.0	44.2	9.0	35.2
1993	55.7	23.7	4.7	27.3	44.3	8.7	35.6
1994	55.3	23.5	4.3	27.6	44.7	8.4	36.3
1995	55.5	23.5	4.0	28.0	44.5	8.4	36.1
1996	57.2	25.9	3.8	27.5	42.8	8.3	34.5
1997	54.7	24.8	4.0	25.9	45.3	8.2	37.1
Costa Rica							
1990	42.3	18.1	5.8	18.4	57.7	22.0	35.7
1991	44.6	19.0	5.6	20.0	55.4	20.3	35.1
1992	41.4	17.6	5.2	18.6	58.6	20.5	38.1
1993	43.7	18.6	5.0	20.1	56.3	20.1	36.2
1994	46.2	17.8	5.3	23.1	53.8	18.4	35.4
1995	44.6	18.1	5.0	21.5	55.4	17.9	37.6
1996	47.2	17.4	5.2	24.6	52.6	17.2	35.4
1997	46.8	18.8	5.4	22.6	53.2	17.0	36.2
Chile							
1990	49.9	23.6	8.1	18.3	50.1	7.0	43.0
1991	49.9	23.1	7.8	19.1	50.1	7.8	42.3
1992	49.7	22.7	7.3	19.6	50.3	8.0	42.3
1993	49.9	22.6	6.6	20.6	50.1	7.9	42.3
1994	51.0	24.2	6.7	20.6	48.4	7.7	40.8
1995	51.2	23.9	6.5	20.8	48.8	7.7	41.1
1996	50.9	22.7	6.8	21.4	49.1	7.6	41.5
1997	51.3	23.0	6.6	21.7	48.7	7.2	41.5
Ecuador							
1990	51.2	32.5	5.6	13.0	48.8	17.6	31.2
1991	54.9	31.5	5.9	17.5	45.1	23.1	22.0
1992	55.1	32.2	6.1	16.8	44.9	14.7	30.2

Country /Year	Informal Sector				Formal Sector		
	Total	Self-Employed[a]	Domestic Service	Small Business[b]	Total	Public Sector	Medium and Large Private Firms
1993	54.1	31.8	5.8	16.5	45.9	13.8	32.0
1994	52.1	30.2	5.8	16.0	47.9	13.7	34.2
1995	53.5	31.3	5.9	16.3	46.5	13.4	33.1
1996	52.9	31.8	5.9	15.2	47.2	13.9	33.3
1997	53.2	30.4	5.4	17.4	46.8	14.8	32.0
Honduras							
1990	54.1	36.3	6.9	10.8	45.9	14.9	31.0
1991	50.7	35.0	6.7	9.0	49.3	16.6	32.7
1992	50.7	35.1	6.7	8.9	49.3	16.4	32.9
1993	45.3	27.5	6.2	11.6	54.7	14.6	40.0
1994	51.8	32.5	5.9	13.4	48.2	12.4	35.9
1995	54.4	34.0	5.4	15.1	45.6	12.5	33.1
1996	56.3	36.5	6.0	13.8	43.6	11.3	32.3
1997	56.6	38.1	5.8	12.7	43.4	10.3	33.1
Mexico							
1990	55.5	30.4	5.6	19.5	44.6	25.0	19.6
1991	55.8	30.5	5.5	19.8	44.2	24.7	19.5
1992	56.0	30.5	5.5	20.0	44.0	24.5	19.5
1993	57.0	30.6	5.5	20.9	43.0	23.0	20.0
1994	57.0	30.7	5.4	20.9	43.0	22.9	20.1
1995	59.4	32.3	5.4	21.7	40.6	22.5	18.1
1996	60.2	32.5	5.4	22.3	39.8	22.0	17.8
1997	59.4	31.2	5.6	22.6	40.6	21.7	18.9
Panama							
1990	40.5	20.4	7.2	12.8	59.5	32.0	27.5
1991	41.2	19.7	7.9	13.6	58.8	27.5	31.3
1992	41.5	19.0	8.5	14.0	58.5	25.2	33.3
1993	39.9	18.2	8.0	13.7	60.1	24.6	35.5
1994	40.2	19.5	7.9	12.9	59.8	24.4	35.4
1995	41.3	20.5	7.6	13.2	58.7	23.4	35.4
1996	41.6	20.7	7.0	13.9	58.3	23.0	35.2
1997	41.5	21.5	7.1	13.0	58.5	21.8	36.6
Paraguay							
1990	61.4	21.2	10.7	29.4	38.6	12.2	26.4
1991	62.0	23.0	10.0	29.0	38.0	11.3	26.7
1992	62.2	22.2	11.0	29.0	37.8	14.6	23.2
1993	62.5	21.5	11.6	29.5	37.5	12.2	25.2
1994	68.9	22.3	11.7	34.9	31.1	11.8	19.3
1995	65.5	25.3	10.6	29.7	34.5	11.9	22.6
1996	67.9	26.9	10.0	31.0	31.1	13.1	19.0
1997	67.9	26.9	10.0	31.0	32.1	13.1	19.0

(Table continues on the following page.)

Table 3.3 (continued)

Country /Year	Informal Sector				Formal Sector		
	Total	Self-Employed[a]	Domestic Service	Small Business[b]	Total	Public Sector	Medium and Large Private Firms
Peru[c]							
1990	51.8	35.3	5.1	11.4	48.2	11.6	36.7
1991	51.8	34.9	4.8	12.1	48.2	11.9	36.3
1992	54.5	37.2	4.9	12.4	45.5	10.0	35.5
1993	54.2	34.7	4.6	14.9	45.8	10.1	35.7
1994	53.8	35.1	4.6	14.1	46.2	7.9	38.3
1995	55.0	35.1	4.7	15.2	45.0	9.1	35.9
1996	57.9	37.4	4.2	16.3	42.1	8.2	33.9
1997	59.3	34.9	5.1	19.4	40.7	7.2	33.5
Uruguay[d]							
1990	36.3	19.3	6.0	11.0	63.7	20.1	43.6
1991	36.7	20.1	6.0	10.6	63.3	18.1	45.2
1992	36.5	20.1	6.3	10.2	63.4	17.5	45.9
1993	37.0	20.6	6.1	11.0	63.0	18.3	44.7
1994	37.9	20.9	6.3	10.7	62.1	16.9	45.2
1995	37.7	21.0	5.9	10.8	62.3	17.7	44.6
1996	37.9	21.3	6.3	10.3	62.1	17.0	45.1
1997	37.1	20.1	6.1	10.9	62.9	16.8	46.1
Venezuela							
1990	38.8	22.1	4.1	12.6	61.2	22.3	38.9
1991	38.3	22.2	3.9	12.2	61.7	21.6	40.1
1992	37.4	22.2	3.4	11.8	62.6	20.2	42.4
1993	38.4	24.1	3.2	11.1	61.6	18.8	42.8
1994	44.8	27.3	3.0	14.5	55.2	19.3	35.9
1995	45.9	27.1	2.3	17.6	53.1	19.5	33.6
1996	47.7	28.1	2.4	17.2	52.3	19.1	33.2
1997	48.1	29.9	2.4	15.8	51.9	19.0	32.9

Note:

[a] Includes self-employed workers (except administrators, professionals, and technicians) and family business workers.

[b] Employed in establishments with fewer than five or ten workers, depending on the available information.

[c] Metropolitan Lima.

[d] Montevideo.

Source: ILO.

Chapter 4
Labor Income and Productivity

During 1990–98, real wages increased (although they declined in a number of countries in 1995, driven mostly by the Mexico devaluation crisis—the "tequila" effect), reversing the trend of the 1980s, when they fell significantly in most countries. Many of the wage increases of 1990–98 have outweighed labor productivity increases in most LAC countries, although a number of countries' wage levels are still below the predebt crisis period. During 1990–98, labor productivity increased by 0.6 percent per year in LAC, while industrial real wages increased by 2.6 percent per year, although it fell by 0.5 percent in 1995, albeit with significant variance across countries (see tables 4.1a and 4.1b, 4.2, and 4.3). By 1998 real wages had reached the levels of 1980. Table 7 shows the yearly changes in average labor productivity for a sample of Latin American countries for the period of study.

However, the variance in wage distribution within each country has been increasing. For example, during 1990–95, Chile's real wages showed sustained increases, with an annual growth rate of 3.8 percent, but did not exceed annual productivity growth, which was 4.1 percent (Leiva 1996). That combination led to increased employment and a reduction in poverty. During the same period, Bolivia secured improvements not only in unemployment, but in real wages as well, with an annual wage growth rate of 3 percent. Peru secured significant job growth and experienced a major increase in real salaries of 30 percent for unskilled labor and 50 percent for skilled labor (Yamada 1996). Differential increases are consistent throughout the region. The premium for skilled workers, and the widening gap relative to unskilled wages, reflects an increase in returns to education, particularly at the tertiary level. Labor markets remain segmented (formal vs. informal) with a relatively small percentage of the labor force enjoying a significantly higher wage than the rest, which is often not justified in terms of productivity. The earnings premiums for formality remain high—in the 20 to 50 percent range on average—but with significant variance. For example, in Mexico, while real wages increased, on average, up to 1994, then falling 23 percent during 1994–97, the proportion of workers earning a below-minimum wage increased as well—to 11.6 percent.

Minimum wages in LAC grew at 1.1 percent per year for the period, with significant variance across countries. Colombia, Costa Rica, Panama, and Paraguay registered the largest increases since 1980, while minimum wages in Argentina (see box 4.1) and Bolivia have increased the most since 1990 (see table 4.4). Similarly, total factor productivity in the 1990s began to recover, with some exceptions, from the significant decreases incurred during the 1980s, as shown in table 4.2. The improvement has been based on greater use of operating capacity, on capital investment, and (mostly) on changes in the organization of production—that is, technical changes of a "disembodied" nature. Table 4.5 shows a breakdown of the contribution. Chile and Colombia, particularly, have surpassed the precrisis levels, due largely to their success in overcoming the external and fiscal deficits and to high levels of investment, which have also surpassed precrisis levels. Selected microdata indicate that most of the factor productivity gains have been concentrated in the manufacturing and utilities sectors (whereas factor productivity appears to have increased little, and even declined, in the service sector).

Box 4.1 Argentina Wage and Productivity Growth (Percentage)

	1990–1994	1991–1994
Cumulative Labor Productivity Growth	21.2	16.0
Cumulative Total Factor Productivity Growth	18.8	11.9
Cumulative Dollar Wage Growth	40.0	33.0
Cumulative Real Wage Growth		
Deflated by Consumer Price Index	28.5	18.1
Deflated by Wholesale Price Index	n/a	45.3

Source: World Bank 1997a.

Table 4.1a Real Wages in Manufacturing in Latin America, 1990–98 (1980 = 100)

	1990	1991	1992	1993	1994	1995	1996	1997	1998	Annual Growth Rate 1990-97	1997-98
Average [a]	87.7	86.9	88.5	90.7	94.2	93.9	94.7	96.9	97.1	1.4	0.2
[b]	84.7	83.4	89.1	92.8	96.4	99.4	100.3	102.8	104.6	2.8	1.8

Note: [a]Simple Average
[b]Weighted Average
Source: ILO on the basis of official figures.

Table 4.1b Average Real Wages in Latin America and the Caribbean

	1980	1985	1989	1990	1991	1992	1993	1994	1995[a]	1996	1997
Average Annual Indexes (1990 = 100)											
Argentina[b]	130.0	135.7	95.5	100.0	101.4	102.7	101.3	102.0	100.9	100.6	100.0
Bolivia[c]	—	64.9	97.6	100.0	93.8	97.6	104.2	112.5	114.2	115.1	—
Brazil[d]	—	—	—	100.0	87.4	77.8	85.9	85.8	88.0	94.1	95.4
Rio de Janeiro	94.0	98.2	111.9	100.0	79.3	79.5	85.7	87.1	91.8	—	—
Sao Paulo	88.6	93.8	111.7	100.0	88.3	85.3	94.6	98.0	102.0	—	—
Chile[e]	95.4	89.3	98.2	100.0	104.9	109.6	113.5	118.8	123.6	128.7	132.2
Colombia[f]	85.0	97.4	101.3	100.0	97.4	98.6	103.2	104.1	105.4	107.0	109.6
Costa Rica[g]	115.6	106.6	98.4	100.0	95.4	99.3	109.5	113.6	111.4	110.4	111.6

(Table continues on the following page.)

Table 4.1b (continued)

	1980	1985	1989	1990	1991	1992	1993	1994	1995ª	1996	1997
Mexico^b	128.3	97.4	96.5	100.0	106.5	114.3	124.5	129.1	111.5	99.2	98.1
Peru^i	309.3	250.2	114.5	100.0	115.2	111.1	110.2	127.4	116.7	111.2	111.0
Uruguay^j	108.5	95.5	107.9	100.0	103.8	106.1	111.2	112.2	109.0	109.7	109.8
Annual Percentage Variation											
Argentina^b	—	—	-19.1	4.7	1.4	1.3	-1.4	0.7	-1.1	-0.3	-0.6
Bolivia^c	—	—	5.7	2.5	-6.2	4.1	6.8	8.0	1.5	0.8	—
Brazil^d	—	—	—	—	-12.6	-11.0	10.4	-0.1	2.6	6.9	1.4
Rio de Janeiro	—	—	1.9	-10.6	-20.7	0.3	7.8	1.6	5.4	—	—
Sao Paulo	—	—	3.4	-10.5	-11.7	-3.4	10.9	3.6	4.1	—	—
Chile^e	—	—	2.0	1.8	4.9	4.5	3.6	4.7	4.0	4.1	2.7
Colombia^f	—	—	1.3	-1.3	-2.6	1.2	4.7	0.9	1.3	1.5	2.4
Costa Rica^g	—	—	0.6	1.7	-4.6	4.1	10.3	3.7	-1.9	-0.9	1.1
Mexico^b	—	—	4.8	3.6	6.5	7.3	8.9	3.7	-13.6	-11.0	-1.1
Peru^i	—	—	-45.1	-12.7	15.2	-3.6	-0.8	15.6	-8.4	-4.7	-0.2
Uruguay^j	—	—	-0.4	-7.3	3.8	2.2	4.8	0.9	-2.9	0.6	0.1

a. Preliminary figures.
b. Average total wages in manufacturing. 1995: January–October average.
c. Wages of workers in private enterprise in La Paz. 1995: Average of March and June.
d. Wages of workers covered by social and labor legislation. 1995: January–July average.
e. Until April 1993, average wages of nonagricultural wage earners. From May 1993 onward, general index of hourly wages. 1995: January–September average.
f. Wages of manual workers in manufacturing. 1995: January–May average.
g. Average remuneration declared by persons covered by the social security system. 1995: January–April average.
h. Average wages in manufacturing. 1995: January–July average.
i. Wages of private sector manual workers in the Lima metropolitan area. 1995: first half of the year.
j. Average salaries. 1995: January–October average.
Source: CEPAL on the basis of official figures.

Table 4.2 Total Factor Productivity Growth

	ARG	BOL	BRA	CHL	COL	GTM	MEX	PRY	PER	VEN
1965–70	−1.0	−0.9	5.6	1.4	1.7	1.4	0.6	−0.6	0.3	0.2
1970–75	−1.6	0.1	5.6	−3.7	1.3	1.0	0.1	0.6	2.2	−1.8
1975–80	−1.4	−1.5	1.9	5.4	1.1	0.4	0.6	1.7	−1.0	−3.0
1980–85	−4.3	−2.4	−1.6	−1.7	−1.9	−3.8	−2.3	−4.4	−2.4	−3.1
1985–90	−1.4	2.0	−0.9	2.4	1.4	0.7	1.4	−0.4	−4.0	0.9
1990–93	5.5	3.0	−0.6	2.8	0.1	0.9	1.2	−1.4	0.3	2.7

Source: Guasch and Monteagudo 1996.

Table 4.3 Average Labor Productivity Growth

	ARG	BOL	BRA	CHL	COL	GTM	MEX	PRY	PER	VEN
90/89	−1.0	2.3	−6.5	1.0	1.6	0.0	1.1	0.2	−7.5	3.6
91/90	7.2	2.0	−1.7	5.4	−0.5	0.4	0.9	−0.4	0.0	7.2
92/91	7.0	0.3	−3.3	9.1	1.9	1.4	−0.3	−1.0	−5.0	2.4
93/92	4.4	1.5	3.1	4.4	2.9	0.6	−2.6	0.9	3.6	−3.3
94/93	5.4	1.6	1.9	2.7	3.3	1.1	0.7	0.7	9.9	−6.1

Source: Guasch and Monteagudo 1996.

Table 4.4 Latin America Urban Real Minimum Wages
(1980 = 100)

Country	1990	1991	1992	1993	1994	1995	1996	1997	Annual Growth Rate 1990–97[d]	1997–98[d]
Argentina[a]	40.2	52.9	45.3	70.0	81.1	78.4	78.3	78.0	9.9	−0.9
Bolivia[a]	16.1	26.3	26.4	28.8	31.7	31.1	31.3	32.2	10.4	15.8
Brazil[a]	65.4	61.8	56.5	63.9	60.8	67.1	68.9	73.2	4.1	3.2
Chile[a]	73.3	79.9	83.4	87.5	90.8	94.8	98.9	102.3	4.9	5.1
Colombia[a]	105.7	103.5	101.8	104.6	102.8	102.4	101.5	103.8	−0.3	−0.6
Costa Rica[b]	127.2	123.3	125.4	130.6	134.6	129.9	130.3	135.0	0.9	4.6
Ecuador	33.9	30.9	33.0	97.8	41.1	49.5	52.3	50.5	5.9	−8.5
El Salvador[b]	33.9	34.6	29.2	35.9	37.3	26.8	33.5	32.0	−0.8	2.7
Guatemala[b]	108.7	99.5	87.5	78.4	74.7	89.3	88.4	80.9	−4.1	5.0
Haití	71.4	67.0	56.8	50.2	39.0	—	—	—	—	—
Honduras[b]	81.9	83.5	100.1	100.9	82.8	80.2	79.5	78.3	−0.6	4.7
México[a]	42.0	39.5	38.3	37.8	37.7	33.3	30.5	30.1	−4.6	−0.6
Panamá[b]	98.4	97.1	95.5	107.2	105.8	105.6	111.4	110.0	1.6	1.5
Paraguay[a]	132.1	125.7	114.7	110.2	113.2	112.8	103.6	107.0	−3.0	−1.0
Perú[a]	21.4	14.9	15.6	12.1	14.4	14.7	15.2	26.7	3.2	18.1

(Table continues on the following page.)

Table 4.4 *(continued)*

Country	1990	1991	1992	1993	1994	1995	1996	1997	Annual Growth Rate 1990– 97[d]	1997– 98[d]
República Dominicana[a]	65.2	78.6	74.7	72.7	73.1	80.3	78.0	—	—	—
Uruguay[a]	68.8	62.9	60.6	51.5	46.0	42.9	41.7	40.8	–7.2	6.0
Venezuela[a]	55.2	61.5	70.2	50.8	52.7	53.7	45.9	39.9	–4.5	10.1
Average[c]	68.4	69.3	67.5	68.4	67.8	70.8	69.9	70.0	0.3	4.1

Note:
a. National minimum wages.
b. Lowest industrial minimum wages.
c. Arithmetic average.
d. Average variation over the January to September periods of each year.
Source: ILO, based on official figures.

Table 4.5 Contributions to GDP Growth

	ARG	BOL	BRA	CHL	COL	GTM	MEX	PRY	PER	VEN
Subperiod 1986–90										
Actual GDP growth (%)	0.283	2.222	1.941	6.588	4.631	2.912	1.38	3.895	–1.757	2.591
Phys. Cap. Contrib. (%)	0.46	–1.02	1.6	2.85	1.94	0.92	1.47	3.01	0.95	0.38
Labor Contrib. (%)	0.047	0.11	0.082	0.084	0.1	0.12	0.125	0.114	0.112	0.125
TFP Contrib. (%)	–0.22	3.13	0.26	3.92	2.59	1.87	–0.22	0.77	–2.82	2.09
Subperiod 1991–93										
Actual GDP growth (%)	7.795	3.83	1.489	8.128	3.77	4.136	2.359	2.618	2.263	5.045
Phys. Cap. Contrib. (%)	1.02	–0.4	0.84	4.08	2.41	1.96	2.28	2.78	0.69	1.09
Labor Contrib. (%)	0.06	0.1	0.085	0.067	0.091	0.131	0.12	0.11	0.111	0.117
TFP Contrib. (%)	6.72	4.13	0.56	3.98	1.27	2.05	–0.04	–0.27	1.46	3.84

Note: TFP = Total factor productivity.
Source: Guasch and Monteagudo 1996.

Chapter 5
Labor Markets and Institutions in Latin American and Caribbean Countries

Undoubtedly, improvement in the employment–unemployment outlook depends on sustained GDP growth rates. Without GDP growth there cannot be much improvement. In a sustained high GDP growth environment, the impact of labor policies, while important, might not be overly determinant (for example, as with the East Asia experience).[8] However, the lagged employment response to sustained high-growth rates implies that their impact on employment is medium to long term. In low- to moderate-growth environments and in transition periods of structural reforms (the LAC environment), however, labor market policies and institutions can significantly affect employment, product, and distributional outcomes. The magnitude of this impact is a nontrivial, empirical question. This book provides some estimates of that impact. Examples such as the U.S. vs. European Union labor market employment performance, the labor market employment performance of the East Asian countries and a number of LAC countries, and the OECD *Jobs Study 1994* are powerful evidence of the impact of labor market policies on employment growth, as illustrated below. Clearly the best course is a mixture of sustained GDP growth and labor reforms that lessens labor protection (in concert[9] with lowering direct and indirect labor costs and decreasing the uncertainty of those costs) and that adds flexibility to labor market transactions, allowing for local, geographical, and firm-specific conditions on employment contracts. The focus of this book is the latter—that is, the impact of labor market structures on employment/unemployment outcomes. We take as a given that all efforts should be focused on securing sustainable economic growth.

Most labor markets in LAC countries are riddled with protection and rigidities that forestall efficiency in the allocation, mobility, and pricing of labor resources. They include highly centralized collective bargaining, restrictions on temporary contracts, high costs for firms in adjusting labor force (inducing high job protection), life-long job security in the public sector, relatively high labor taxes, noncompetitive wage determination mechanisms, direct government intervention in the wage-setting mechanism, disincentives for performance-based compensation, and inefficient conflict-resolution schemes. Labor market policies and institutions in LAC countries have often been designed as instruments for social policy, rather than as instruments to secure efficiency in the allocation and mobility of labor and to provide appropriate signals for the investment in human capital. Their design as primarily social policy instruments has tended to ignore the often perverse incentives of such design, securing neither an efficient allocation of labor resources nor an effective social outcome.

Job protection laws in many Latin American countries are attempting to achieve two policy objectives with the same instrument: penalizing wrongful dismissals and providing unemployment insurance, for example. The problem is that neither objective is well served. Firms devise ways of reducing the costs of mandated severance payments, and employees attempt to transform voluntary departures into dismissals in order to receive severance payments. The law has the effect of making labor a quasi-fixed factor. As a result, hiring and firing decisions are not optimal and are also subject to delays, informality increases, and most temporary contracts are informal (World Bank 1995). More effective and less counterproductive instruments than labor market rigidities exist to achieve social objectives. Labor market policies that appear to protect low-income workers encourage inflexibility (especially at the low end of the labor market) and long-term unemployment. Generous income support acts as a floor on wages and discourages low-income job creation, as demonstrated by the performance of labor markets in European Union countries, described below, and the rising economic informality in LAC. Faced with adverse shocks, a labor welfare policy that ignores labor market incentives can be more costly in terms of lost jobs, output, and financial costs than a policy that does not. When protections and rigidities are in place, the market responds to shocks with weaker labor demand and increased informality, rather than reduced poverty or unemployment, which are often highly correlated, as the Chilean case demonstrates.

Chapter 6
Factors Affecting Labor Demand

The main engine of employment growth (labor demand) is overall economic growth. But the relationship between employment growth and output growth is greatly affected by the efficiency and institutional structure of the labor market, via the impact of labor costs, broadly understood. Specifically, labor demand is affected by the level of economic activity (GDP growth) and of unit labor costs (absolute and relative to others factors of production). This chapter reviews the current causes of high labor costs and opportunities for lowering them, with the understanding that economic growth is essential in order to increase labor demand and to realize the medium- to long-term benefits of labor market reforms. Reduced labor costs also favorably affect growth through output cost reductions, increased competitiveness and productivity, reduced product prices, and increased product demand. The other critical factor affecting labor demand (and wages) is the labor force's skill level, which is developed through a strategic educational investment policy. Such investments should be pursued vigorously, although their benefits are realized only in the longer term, and their magnitude depends on the degree to which the demand for skills in the labor market reflects global and domestic competitive pressures.

Labor costs have two major components—wages and non-wage-related costs. Wage levels can be made more flexible through increased competition in the labor market (for example, greater contractual freedom and decentralized collective bargaining). Nonwage costs include labor taxes, other legal remunerations (paid vacations, year-end bonuses, and so on), and transaction costs associated with adjusting employment levels. Labor taxes or fiscal obligations entail social security and health contributions, which ostensibly serve to pay for services provided usually by the government. Parafiscal obligations, such as mandated training expenses and housing finance fees in some countries, also exist. Labor taxes do not accrue directly to the worker, but rather are intermediated by a public institution and thus introduce a wedge between the benefit perceived by workers and the cost of labor. To the extent that non-wage labor costs introduce a tax wedge between the benefits received by workers and the costs paid by firms, non-wage labor costs create a deadweight loss. By the same token, they create an arbitrage opportunity for firms and workers to split this loss by withdrawing from the formal sector. Table 6.1 shows the high levels of those

29

Table 6.1 Composition of Total Labor Costs and Tax Wedge* in Selected Latin American Countries, 1980–95 (in Percentages, Expressed as Proportion of Gross Remuneration)

| Country/ Year | Worker Contribution | Employer Contribution | | | Total Labor Cost | Tax Wedge = Fiscal Cont. ÷ (100 + legal benefits) |
		Legally Mandated Benefits	Fiscal Contributions			
Mexico						
1980	5.1	21.6	19.0		140.6	15.6
1990	5.1	21.6	25.2		146.8	20.7
1995	5.1	21.6	27.4		149.0	22.5
Argentina						
1980	14.0	23.5	43.9		167.4	35.5
1990	16.0	23.3	40.4		163.7	32.8
1995	17.0	21.4	27.2		148.6	22.4
Brazil						
1990	9.0	22.4	35.8		158.2	29.2
1995	9.0	22.4	35.8		158.2	29.2
Chile						
1990	21.1	34.1	10.4		144.5	7.8
1995	21.1	34.1	10.4		144.5	7.8
Peru						
1990	6.0	30.0	30.8		160.8	23.7
1995	11.4	30.0	32.9		162.9	25.3

Sources: Tokman and Martinez 1997, and World Bank 1998.

* This tax wedge can be conceptualized analytically in the following demand and supply framework: denote the demand for labor as $Ld = A[w(1+t)]^a$ and the supply of labor as $Ls = A[w(1+xt)]^b$, where w is the net wage received by workers and t is the fiscal contribution paid by firms (and expressed as share of the net wage). These fiscal contributions serve to finance certain benefits that accrue to workers and the variable x, which assumes a value between 0 and 1, denotes the share of those tax payments that the worker perceives as a net benefit. Now note in a market clearing context that a change in the tax, t, influences the equilibrium wage and employment as follows:

$$dL/L = abt(1-x)/(b-a) \qquad dw/w = (a-bx)t/(b-a), \qquad \text{where } a<0, b>0.$$

From these expressions, if $x = 1$ (meaning that workers perceive the fiscal contributions as fully part of their remuneration; as in the case of legally-mandated benefits), then the market clearing wage declines by the full amount of the fiscal contribution ($dw/w = -t$) and there is no change in employment ($dL/L = 0$). At the other extreme, if $x = 0$ (meaning that the fiscal contributions are perceived as merely a tax disassociated from any benefits), then the wage falls by less than the rise in fiscal contributions and employment declines, or rather, workers have a greater incentive to establish an informal working arrangement where the firm does not make the fiscal contribution and the worker suffers no wage decline.

costs and tax wedges for selected Latin American countries. Non-wage costs to employers can be lowered through a reduction in labor taxes and transaction costs (severance and compensation payments), at the same time lowering the uncertainty associated with the latter. A third element—productivity—also has an impact on effective or unit labor costs, since any increase in labor productivity decreases unit labor costs. The impact of productivity gains actually works, through decreased labor costs and increased GDP growth. But it depends on how or who appropriates the productivity gains. Productivity gains reduce unit labor costs. If those reductions are fully or partially passed to output prices, lowering output demand will increase and through that there will be the corresponding employment growth. If output prices are not affected, and productivity gains not fully absorbed in wage increases, there will be employment growth, since marginal product of labor has increased. If on the other hand the productivity gains are fully converted in wage increases, there will be little direct impact on employment.

The key mechanisms by which labor markets affect labor demand through labor costs are, more specifically, the following:

Direct and indirect costs of labor. This refers to wage levels, labor taxes, and other imputed costs such as absenteeism, nonworking days, accident liabilities, and imputed compensations. Mandated payroll contributions as a percentage of gross wages range (adding to the wage bill) from 22 to 45 percent for LAC countries, with Argentina, Brazil, Peru, and Uruguay in the lead. Many of those rates are high by international standards (see figure 6.1), and even more important, have little connection with the benefits that labor taxes are supposed to provide to workers. The effective tax is actually even higher because of the other costs associated with current labor regulations, such as effective hours worked, paid vacations, year-end bonuses, severance liabilities, and insurance costs. When imputations are made to reflect these implicit costs, the effective tax rate rises to almost 60 percent for the top countries. In many LAC countries, payroll taxes are to a large extent a source of fiscal resources, rather than an instrument to provide corresponding benefits to workers; clearly they induce distortions in the choice of inputs for production. The evidence of the adverse effects of high payroll taxes on employment is quite large and consistent as table 6.2 shows.

Contractual flexibility. This mechanism is used to determine the level and structure of wages; it includes contractual modes laws, labor/management relations, and the structure of collective bargaining. Wage and contractual flexibility is constrained in a number of LAC countries by nu-

Figure 6.1 Labor Taxes (as Percentage of Gross Wages)

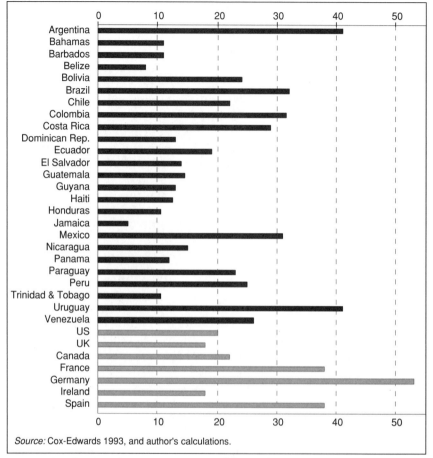

Source: Cox-Edwards 1993, and author's calculations.

merous institutional arrangements. Table 6.3 describes the industrial relations systems in selected LAC countries, and tables 6.4 and 6.5 illustrate
the region's underlying labor law clauses. The most salient factors affecting labor market flexibility are:

(a) The highly centralized collective bargaining structure (legally granted
monopoly power over negotiations in the hands of sector unions) and ergo
omnes clauses (labor laws that give extraordinary bargaining power and influence on market conditions to "representative unions," allowing them to
negotiate conditions that apply both to their own enterprise and to the competition). Centralized collective bargaining predominates in Argentina, Brazil, Mexico, and Uruguay. A similar effect is produced by administrative
extensions, which extend collective bargaining agreements to the entire sector and are common in the region. Representation is guaranteed by the affiliation of large numbers of workers with the union. This means that large

Table 6.2 OECD: Employment Effects of Changes in Payroll Tax Rates

Country Study	Result
UK-a (1986)	13 percentage point rise in taxes increases unemployment by 1.4 percentage points.
UK-b (1987)	Increase in payroll taxes increased real wages in the short term, so likely reduced employment immediately.
UK-c (1993)	Increase in payroll taxes led to increase in unemployment.
Canada (1990)	Payroll taxes have increased structural unemployment by 2.5 percentage points.
Denmark (1990)	Increase in payroll taxes increased real wages by the same amount, implying a fall in employment.
Norway (1990, 1988, 1989)	10% increase in payroll taxes increased wages between 8-10%, implying a fall in employment.
Denmark and Norway (1990)	Increase in payroll taxes increased real wages in the short term only; no long term effect on employment.
Finland (1990)	Small long-term impact on wages and employment.
Finland and Norway (1985)	Increase in payroll taxes increased real wages in the short term only; on long term effect on employment.
Italy (1990)	Increase in payroll taxes led to increase in unemployment.
Spain (1986)	Significant effect on real wages and thus reduced employment.
OECD-a (1986)	Increase in payroll taxes responsible for about 50% of the increase in unemployment.
OECD-b (1991)	Significant effect on real wages, and so reduced employment.

Source: OECD Employment Outlook (1998)

enterprises or highly concentrated sectors are likely to be the core of union activity, and that representation is oriented toward the interests of workers in large enterprises. Enterprise unions are often discouraged by law, and they tend to exist mostly in monopolistic sectors. In a number of LAC countries, labor laws establish that union contributions agreed upon by *convenio* are required from all workers covered by an agreement, and that employers must deduct them. This means that while affiliation is optional, contributions to the union movement are obligatory and agreements apply to all workers covered, independent of their participation or representation in the negotiation process or in the election of leaders (the *ergo omnes* principle).[10] The legal framework in a number of LAC countries makes unionization a sector choice. The decision is not made at the firm or individual level. Often, the law also establishes that collective agreements signed between employers and workers covered by the *convenios* described above cannot contradict the conditions established by those *convenios*.[11]

(Text continues on page 39.)

Table 6.3 Comparing Industrial Relations Systems in Six Latin American Countries

	General Characteristics	State Intervention	Centralization/Decentralization
Argentina	Centralized, strong state intervention. Recent efforts to decentralize.	State confers union status (*personería gremial* [PG]) determining who bargains; labor ministry present throughout process. All agreements must be registered with administrative authority. Homologation powerful tool by state to stipulate bargaining; considers impact of agreement on economy and consumers. 1994 Constitution recognizes executive's power to rescind collective agreement or parts thereof for economic emergency. State determines legality of strikes and presides in mandatory conciliation of disputes and can impose mandatory arbitration.	Legislation centralizes system; firm-level unions can only receive PG if no sector-level union. Monopoly representation by unions w/ PG who represent affiliated and nonaffiliated workers. 7% of unions represent 75% of workers. Most bargaining at higher level; 70% of collective agreements by activity or branch. Recent reform to decentralize would allow parties to modify level of negotiations, and if disagreement, labor ministry settles dispute, defaulting to lower level.
Brazil	Centralized, high state intervention mitigated by 1988 Constitution. Still considered corporatist, though now toward collective autonomy and	1988 Constitution protects union autonomy; state no longer able to confer union status or intervene in union administration. However, intervention still exists but enforced through Labor Courts. Bargaining process not regulated, though product is. State continues to invoke old labor code declaring arbitration through *dissidio* process in cases of essential services. *Dissidio* pro-	1988 Constitution maintained corporatist structure. Only one union with *sindicato* status can represent a profession by industry in geographic territory. The law does not allow for firm-based unions. *Sindicatos* can bargain at firm or sector level, often pursuing a bilevel strategy to avoid the salary limits imposed by government policy. Trend toward decentralization. 1988 Constitution provides that rect negotiations with employer.

Brazil *(continued)*	autonomy and efforts to decentralize by unions and employers.	cess in cases of essential services. *Dissisio* process triggers mandatory conciliation and arbitration by tripartite Labor Courts.	
Chile	Decentralized, mixed state intervention; recuperation of collective autonomy with return to democratization, but still intervention in conflict resolution.	Unions do not need state approval to form, but process is regulated, as is internal administration. Unions report yearly to state. Bargaining process highly regulated but allows autonomy in negotiations. Also, "unregulated bargaining" process but does not carry strike option. Agreements cannot limit employer's "ability to organize, control, and administer the firm." Parties can opt for voluntary mediation or arbitration at any time during bargaining. State can impose mandatory arbitration to end "abusive strike." Strike process regulated in detail.	Most unions at firm level. Constitution protects only firm-level bargaining. More than 1 union can exist per firm and sign own collective agreement. 1991 reform allows multiemployer bargaining (unless enterprise subsidized more than 50% by state) to improve coverage rates, but process considered too restrictive. Also established right to organize fourth-level national trade union organization, *centrales*. Social consultation important in transition to democracy.

(Table continues on the following page.)

Table 6.3 *(continued)*

	General Characteristics	State Intervention	Centralization/Decentralization
Mexico	Centralization achieved through corporatist structure and union discipline; high state intervention.	Main intervention through state registration of unions and in strikes. Independent or other unions outside the corporatist structure frequently not registered and strikes suppressed. Exclusion and separation clauses maintain system. Bargaining autonomy undermined by employers who satisfy duty to sign by signing minimum agreements ("contracts of protection"). State intervenes in conflict resolution through conciliation and arbitration boards and by declaring strikes nonexistent. Negotiation process not highly regulated, but integrated with conflict resolution (usually occurs in conciliation) in which there is high state intervention.	Different types of unions allowed, though most firm level. Union with majority represents all workers in firm. Highly disciplined syndical movements achieve coordination in bargaining. Industrywide contracts must be approved by labor ministry, but few signed. Tripartite bargaining and *pactos sindicales* play integral role in economic restructuring.

| Peru | Decentralized, high state intervention. System reformed in 1992 to increase direct negotiation and decrease state intervention. | Main intervention through registration of unions and conflict resolution. 1992 reform establishes that unions can be denied registration only for noncompliance with legal requirements. Improved room for direct negotiations. Post-1992 reform agreements do not need state approval. But 1991 decree prohibits collective agreement from granting wage indexation in state enterprises, replacing existing clauses with mechanisms that take into account productivity. And state can still intervene to review demands and economic records. Conflict-resolution procedures reformed to increase direct negotiations. Previously, bargaining system was rigid, procedural, and trial-like, designed for resolution by administrative decision if no agreement after 8 days mandatory conciliation. Now, conciliation process is more flexible. 1992 strike regulated in detail. Labor ministry can mandate conciliation and arbitration if strike lasts too long and threatens firm or sector. | Decentralized. Firm-based unions dominate (97.42% at firm level, only 2.4% industrywide). 1992 reform allowed more than 1 union per firm; most representative union has monopoly on representation. Workers can represent selves if no union organized. Parties choose level of agreement; if no consensus, defaults to firm level. Almost all agreements signed at firm level. |

(Table continues on the following page.)

Table 6.3 *(continued)*

	General Characteristics	State Intervention	Centralization/Decentralization
Uruguay	Centralized, low state intervention.	Since 1985 repeal of syndical legislation, collective bargaining system "unregulated." No law defines or requires registration of unions, or governs collective bargaining or conflict resolution. Mutual good faith that agreements will be abided by underlies system. During conflicts, unions mainly self-regulating through provisions in their charters or collective agreements.	Some firm-based unions, but most industrywide because evolved within old framework of tripartite Wage Councils. Most bargaining sectorwide. If more than one union exists and they do not agree to negotiate jointly, "most representative union" bargains. Social consultation important in transition to democracy.

Source: Inter-American Development Bank 1998.

Overall, such an environment hinders wage flexibility and efficient responses, to the detriment of employment, since it does not allow a firm to respond unilaterally to changing local and general economic conditions in terms of its wage offers. The adverse impact of centralized collective bargaining in job creation can be quite significant, as shown below. Decentralization of collective bargaining at the firm level would also produce a greater wage dispersion, essential to foster vigorous job creation, as illustrated by the OECD experience reported below. Moreover, not surprisingly, the highly centralized collective bargaining structure tends to lead to gains for employed union members, often at the expense of other workers' income—that is, nonunion, informal, and unemployed workers—rather than at the expense of firms' profits, as is often argued.

(b) Restrictions on the modes of contracting, particularly limitations on temporary or fixed-term contracts and on part-time contracts, reduce the flexibility of firms to use labor efficiently. Such restrictions are common in most LAC countries. While their broad use, if allowed, does induce some substitutability, their impact on net employment is positive and especially affects youth and unskilled employment. In addition, while not barred by legislation, broadly based incentive pay remuneration (a concern in many LAC countries) is lacking, in contrast to the extensive use of performance-based compensation in East Asian countries. Often the cause has been poor labor/management relations and union resistance. Yet the evidence of the positive impact of incentive pay is overwhelming. Where used, significant productivity gains have followed, often in the 15 to 35 percent range; usually, over half of the worker-specific increases in productivity have been passed on to workers in the form of higher wages. Incentive pay remuneration also leads, not surprisingly, to higher dispersion of workers' earnings—a frequent concern to the unions (Fama 1991; Lazear 1996; Paarsch and Shearer 1996).

(c) Job security and labor stability clauses significantly increase the cost of labor force adjustments, either directly or through the uncertainty of their final value, due to the often accompanying litigation process. Most labor law in LAC countries offers significant job security, especially as established by labor stability laws, with no distinction between just cause and unjust cause dismissal. And even when the law establishes that distinction, economic causes such as a drop in an individual firm demand or a low productivity of a worker are considered unjust cause dismissals. The laws also provide high levels of compensation in the event of dismissal (see tables 6.4 and 6.5). Imputed direct costs of layoffs range from 6 to 12 percent of the monthly wage bill (World Bank 1998; Guasch, Gill, and Pessino 1996). However, due to the litigation process accompanying the layoffs, significant added costs and uncertainty over the final total costs exist. Direct and indirect litigation costs must be added to the cost of labor force adjustments (often increasing base costs by 30 percent), since most dismissals tend to end up in labor courts, which traditionally

(Text continues on page 46.)

Table 6.4 Firing Conditions and Job Protection Laws in Latin American Countries, 1995 (X = Monthly Salary; N = Years Worked)

Country	Reform Date	Period of Notification	Payment for Firing with Just Cause	Payment for Firing Without Just Cause	Firing Due to Economic Conditions	Limit on Payment for Firing	Compensation in Case of Resigning	Restrictions on Temporary Contracts	Probationary Period
Argentina	1991	1 month	0	1 x *N. Min. 2 months.	½ x *N. Min. 2 months	Lim. Max. in x	No	2 years, nonrenewable	3 months
Bahamas	None	½–1 month	0	Negotiated between the employee and the employer. Legislation does not stipulate an amount.	Negotiable	No	No	WR – 1 year	3 months
Barbados	None	Negotiable. In practice 1 month.	0	2 ½ wks. if 1, N<=10; 3 wks, if 10<N>20; 3 ½ wks. if N>20	2 ½ wks. if N<=10; 3 wks, if 10<N>20; 3 ½ wks. if N>20	Lim. Max. in x	No	WR	Negotiable
Belize	None	½–1 month	0	After N=5, the employee has the right to 1 wk. pay of salary per year worked.	Idem	Max. 42 wks.	From N=10¼ *N	WR	2 weeks
Bolivia	None	3 months	0	1 x *N	1 x *N	No	From 5th year 1 x*N	Renewable once	3 months

40

Country	Year	Notice	FUND	Severance	Severance	Max	Fund	Contract	Period
Brazil	None	1 month	FUND	1.4 FUND	1.4 FUND	No	FUND	2 years, nonrenewable	12 months
Chile	None	1 month	0	1.2 x *N[a]	1 x *N	Max. N=11	From the 7th year ½ x*N[b]	1 year, nonrenewable	12 months
Colombia	1990	45 days	FUND, without retirement	FUND+x*4.2 if N=5;x*13.5 if N=10;x*20.2 if N=15;x*21.8 if N=20	FUND+x*4.2 if N=5;x*13.5 if N=10;x*20.2 if N=15;x*21.8 if N=20	No	FUND	3 years	2 months
Costa Rica	None	1 month	0	x *N	x *N	Max. N=8	No	WR	3 months
Dom. Rep.	None	½–1 month	0		½–1 x *N	No	No		3 months
Ecuador	None	1 month	FUND +¼ x *N	¼ x *N+FUND + 3*x if N<3; x *N if 3<N<25; pension if N>25	¼ x *N+FUND + 3*x if N<3; x *N if 3<N<25; pension if N>25	No	FUND	2 years, nonrenewable	3 months
El Salvador	1994	0–7 days	0	x*N. Change in the lim. max indemnified	0 if due to bankruptcy; x *N otherwise	Sal. max 4 min. salaries	No		1 month
Guatemala	1991	No	0	1 mth/year worked. Dep. on FUND. Fund+Interest	2 days–4 mths if bankruptcy, otherwise Fund+Interest	No	No		2 months
Guyana	None	1/2 month	0	Negotiated in collective conv., 2 ½ x N in practice	Negotiable	No	No	WR	None
Haiti	None	2–12 weeks	0			No	No		
Honduras	None	1 day 2 months	0	x *N	x *N	Max. N=15	No	WR	2 months
Jamaica	None	2–12 weeks	0			No	No	WR	3 months

(Table continues on the following page.)

Table 6.4 (continued)

Country	Reform Date	Period of Notification	Payment for Firing with Just Cause	Payment for Firing Without Just Cause	Firing Due to Economic Conditions	Limit on Payment for Firing	Compensation in Case of Resigning	Restrictions on Temporary Contracts	Probationary Period
Mexico	None	0–1 month	x*3	⅔ x*N	²/₃ x *N	No	No	no restrictions	None
Nicaragua		1–2 month	x*N	2 x*N	2 x *N	No		2 years, nonrenewable	12 months
Paraguay	None	1–2 month	0	½ x*N^c	½ x N*c	No	No	3 months	1–2 months
Peru	1995, 1991	No	FUND	FUND+x*N	FUND+x*N	Max. N=12	FUND	2 years, nonrenewable	3 months
Suriname	None	¼–6 month	0	Trial result in favor of employee	Idem^d	No	No	WR	2 months
Trin. & Tob.	None	2 month	0	½ x *N if 1<N>4; ¾ x *N if N>5	½ x *N if 1<N>4; No ¾ x *N if N>5	No	No	WR	Negotiable
Uruguay	None	No	x*N	x*N	x*N	Max. N=6	No		3 months
Venezuela	None	⅓–3 month	⅓–1 x *N	⅔–2 x*N	⅔–2 x*N	No	⅓–1x*N	renewable once	3 months

a. If the employer cannot prove "economic cause," there is a charge of 20 percent. If the employer cannot prove "just cause," the charge is 50 percent.
b. The workers can demand one month per year in case of being fired, or one-half month per year under any circumstances, after the seventh year.
c. Prohibited to fire employees who have been working for the company for more than 10 years.
d. Payment made only if it is determined by a legal procedure. Economic conditions are considered just cause.
WR = Without Restrictions.

Source: Marquez 1994, Cox-Edwards 1993, and author's calculations.

Table 6.5 Dispute Resolution

Country	Judicial Procedure Rests On	Right of Employees		To Renounce Union Membership and Go Back to Work	Right of Employers		Maximum Duration of a Strike
		To Strike	To Wage Replacement		To Lock-Out	To Temporarily Replace Workers	
Argentina	Civil Courts	Must be called by union. After conciliation channels are exhausted. Ministry of Labor pronounces legality.	NO, if workers fail to accept arbitration. YES, of the employer locks out workers.	NO	NO, unless the strike is illegal.	NO	No maximum
Bolivia	Labor Courts	After arbitration process has failed (requires at least 24 days after presentation of petition to labor inspector). The majority of union or ⅔ of workers must agree.	NO. Strike suspends labor contracts.	YES	YES	NO	No maximum. In spite of the law, many strikes start before the Tribunal decision.

(Table continues on the following page.)

Table 6.5 (continued)

Country	Right of Employees				Right of Employers		
	Judicial Procedure Rests On	To Strike	To Wage Replacement	To Renounce Union Membership and Go Back to Work	To Lock-Out	To Temporarily Replace Workers	Maximum Duration of a Strike
Brazil	Labor Courts	YES, in the context of collective contract negotiations. Quorum requirement to be decided by union. Decided by head-count vote.	NO	YES Strike does not suspend contract.	Requires prior authorization.	NO, unless the strike is declared abusive by the Court.	No maximum
Colombia	Labor Courts. Within 2 days of declared strike, the Ministry of Labor may call for an arbitration.	After direct negotiations period. Must be agreed to on a secret ballot by absolute majority of enterprise workers.	NO. Strike suspends labor contracts.	NO		NO, unless there is a risk of serious damage to the facilities.	60 days
Chile	Labor Courts have jurisdiction over questions arising out of the application of the law.	YES, in the context of collective contracts negotiations.	NO	YES	YES, if the strike affects more than 50% of workers. YES, if the strike leads to stoppage	YES, from the first day of the strike if the last offer is equivalent to the previous	If more than half of the workers have returned to work the strike ends.

					of essential work.	contract adjusted by CPI. Only after 15 days, otherwise.	
Ecuador	Labor Inspectorate	If direct negotiations fail, as long as the absolute majority of workers agrees. "Solidarity" strikes permitted.	YES	NO	NO	NO	Once the tribunal resolves, the strike ends.
Mexico	Labor Courts	Tripartite Board must declare it "existent" or legal.	NO, unless the Board decides the strike is "imputable" to the employer.	NO	NO		No maximum
Nicaragua	Civil Courts	YES, if agreed by head count majority. Does not have to occur in the context of collective bargaining.	YES	Workers can go back to work. But wages are paid anyway.	YES. After conciliation. If authorized by Labor Inspectorate.	Prohibited	No maximum
Peru	Ministry of Labor	YES, if the majority approves. Very few limitations.	NO. Strike suspends labor contracts.	Not regulated	NO	Not regulated	No maximum
Venezuela	Labor Inspectorate	If direct negotiations fail, as long as the absolute majority of workers agrees. "Solidarity" strikes permitted.	NO. Strike suspends labor contract.	NO	Not regulated	Not regulated	No maximum

Source: Cox-Edwards 1995.

favor labor over management, regardless of the merits of the case. Those litigation costs can bring—and have brought—a number of firms, particularly small firms, to bankruptcy.

(d) In a number of LAC countries, no workmen's compensation insurance in the event of a labor-related accident has been established. The consequences of such a lack are high costs to the firm, mostly resulting from costly and uncertain litigation, with most of the expenses going to lawyers and experts. Adopting a modern workmen's compensation insurance scheme can reduce these costs significantly, and thus increase jobs. For example, in Argentina, the imputed costs to firms before adoption of a national insurance system was 8 percent of the wage bill. After an insurance law was enacted, insurance premiums, through competition among providers, fell on average to 1.5 percent of the wage bill.

(e) While in most LAC countries minimum wages are nonbinding, in a number of countries, such as Colombia, Ecuador, and Mexico, governments do affect the general level of wages through administrative links. Direct government intervention further tampers with the competitive wage-determination process, as in Ecuador, through periodic, mandated across-the-board wage increases, indexation, or minimum wage changes. In Colombia, the government intervenes through administratively linking the minimum wage to the general level of wages.

Thus, an increase in the minimum wage or indexation automatically increases the general level of wages. Since workers cannot be paid above their marginal contribution to production, these forms of government intervention can result in fewer jobs. This should not be misconstrued to say that governments should not intervene in labor markets. Indeed, a role exists for government intervention, but it should be limited to the establishment and protection of workers' rights, such as the right to associate and organize, to bargain collectively, and to engage in an industrial-action strike; the protection of the vulnerable through a minimum working age, equality of wages and employment opportunities, and special provision for women; establishment of minimum compensation for work, through minimum wages and minimum non-wage benefits and overtime pay; assurance of decent and safe working conditions; and provision of income security through social security and severance payments or unemployment insurance, and emergency public works programs.

(f) Performance-based compensation is hardly used in the region. Most of the collective labor contracts do not provide for that type of wage flexibility. For example, in Mexico only 16 percent of labor contracts do (World Bank 1998), and similar percentages exist in Argentina, Brazil, and Uruguay. Additionally, in a number of LAC countries, institutional elements discourage the use of performance-based worker compensation. The normative scheme in those countries is to include any productivity bonus in the computation of severance payments in the event of separation, thus increasing the imputed cost of labor. This disincentive, along with the traditional reluctance of unions to negotiate compensation leading to wage variance within a job classification, is to some extent responsible for the limited use of performance-based worker compensation in LAC countries. The result is an adverse impact on productivity and labor demand. (For a determination of the efficiency of wage-productivity gaps, see Guasch and Weiss 1981, 1982.)

3. *Quality and skill level of the labor force.* The key factors affecting the quality of the labor force are levels of education and training; both are lacking in LAC countries. In 1987, the average level of schooling among 15- to 64-year-olds was 5.6 years, which is deficient regardless even of the quality of the education obtained. (Figure 6.2 shows the average years of schooling among adults aged 18 and older for selected countries in the region). The average (private) expenditure on training in the region is below 0.5 percent of the wage bill—again, a deficient number by most standards. These factors determine the value of labor to entrepreneurs, and thus affect the level of economic activity.

Figure 6.2 Average Years of Schooling Among Adults Aged 18 and Older in Selected LAC Countries

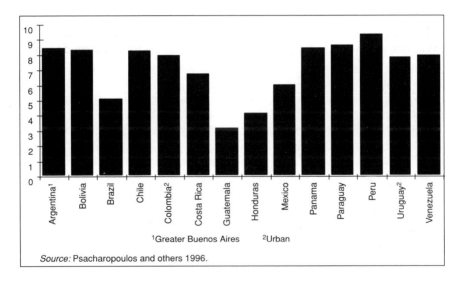

[1]Greater Buenos Aires   [2]Urban

Source: Psacharopoulos and others 1996.

Chapter 7
Remedies to Address the Employment Issue

Components of a Package of Comprehensive Reforms

The solution to the employment–unemployment problem is obviously increased labor demand, which itself will rise with greater economic activity and reduced labor costs. The demand response to change in those two factors is given by the output and wage elasticities, respectively. The wage elasticity of labor demand provides an estimate of the employment increase that can be expected from labor market reforms that lower the price of labor relative to capital and other factors. The output elasticity of labor demand, holding wages and other labor costs constant, provides a quantitative estimate of how much employment can be expected to increase with renewed output growth if labor market policy remains unchanged. While sustained high economic growth is essential to reduce unemployment over the medium to long term (and, arguably, is also sufficient, as the East Asia experience might indicate), labor policy reforms can both reduce unemployment in the shorter term, ensuring a stronger linkage between output and employment growth, and be particularly effective in low- to moderate-growth environments, such as LAC countries. Moreover, the usual estimates of those elasticities in most countries show a stronger labor demand response to reductions in labor costs than to increases in growth. The labor cost elasticity (–0.80 to –0.30) usually tends to be twice the value of the output elasticity (0.15 to 0.5). For example, Guasch, Gill, and Pessino (1996) estimated Argentina's labor cost elasticity to be 0.5, while the estimate of its output elasticity was 0.25 (see tables 7.1 and 7.2). Moreover, not surprisingly, a correlation appears to exist between those elasticities and the degree of labor market flexibility (OECD *Jobs Study 1994*). That is, the more flexible the labor market is, the more responsive employment growth is to output growth and labor cost reductions. The argument is that the lower the costs to adjust labor levels, the more firms are likely to respond to increases in output demand by hiring additional workers. Thus, reducing labor costs has both a direct effect, through wage elasticity, and a significant indirect effect, through increases in the output elasticity.

48

Table 7.1 Wage Elasticities and Employment Response

Country	Wage Elasticity	Medium Lag (years)
Argentina	–0.5	3.0
United States	–1.0	1.0
Japan	–0.8	3.0
Germany	–1.0	2.0
France	–1.0	2.0
Italy	–0.5	5.0
United Kingdom	–1.0	4.0
Canada	–0.5	1.0
Australia	–1.0	2.0
Sweden	–0.9	7.0
Finland	–1.0	3.0

Source: OECD *Jobs Study 1994*; and Guasch, Gill, and Pessino 1996.

Table 7.2 Estimates of Long-run Output Elasticities

Country	Output Elasticity
Argentina	0.25
United States	0.41
Germany	0.34
Canada	0.45
France	0.32
Italy	0.11
Japan	0.10
United Kingdom	0.57
Spain	0.44
Australia	0.51
Norway	0.25
Austria	0.18

The coefficients are derived from individual country equations.
Source: Revenga and Bentolila 1994, and Guasch, Gill, and Pessino 1996.

Reducing Labor Costs

In the short run, as the discussion so far has shown, only a reduction in labor costs (i.e., an increase in labor market flexibility) will significantly improve the employment/unemployment outlook. Such a reduction can come from two sources: (a) lowering payroll taxes and other indirect labor costs and (b) eliminating existing institutional rigidities that hinder wage flexibility. This section points out the opportunities to reduce labor costs, and assesses the potential impact of making the wage determination process more competitive (for example, by decentralizing the collective bargaining process), based on experience in other countries and simulations.

Lowering Payroll Taxes

The relatively high levels of payroll taxes in the region and their weak link to benefits (to workers) suggest that there is some room for an efficient reduction of payroll taxes to stimulate labor demand. Given the standard wage (labor costs) elasticity of employment, payroll tax reductions (incidence issues aside) can have a significant impact on employment. However, lowering these taxes has a cost: the adverse fiscal impact.

Tax reductions typically have a negative effect on tax revenues in the short run, because the lower tax rate applies to the initial payroll and to any additional employment induced by the lower tax. For example, given a wage elasticity of –0.5, a 10 percent reduction in labor taxes will induce a revenue reduction of 5.5 percent.[12] However, fiscal benefits result as well. First, if a sizable number of workers newly employed as a result of the tax reduction had been receiving unemployment benefits at the current replacement rates, the impact on net revenues could be positive. Second, a lower tax rate tends to induce an increase in employment, encourages the formalization of labor contracts, and increases compliance. This in turn increases the tax base, and in that way increases tax collections. Studies for other countries have shown that the probability of such a reduction contributing to the system is inversely related to the tax rate, and that the revenue-maximizing tax rate is often below the actual rate. This was the case in Brazil during 1982–91, and in Argentina, where prior to the tax increases in the early 1980s, the noncompliance rate was estimated at 18.7 percent. With the payroll tax increases, noncompliance estimates rose to 23.7 percent in 1986 and 27.6 percent in 1990.[13]

Employment Cost of the Current Severance System

Severance's financial cost also needs to be recognized as a barrier to employment growth. While a need exists to provide some financial support to unemployed workers, the current structure is very inefficient. Under the current system, on terminating an employee without "just cause," the employer must pay a severance indemnity ranging from two weeks' to two months' salary (at least) for each year of service, based on the highest salary level during the last year of employment, often with a minimum of two months' compensation plus one month for prenotification. In some countries, the severance payment may be prefunded on a tax-advantageous basis through a book reserve of that amount. The employer's liability in cases of dismissal is a function of tenure and wages. The continuous increase in employer's liability as tenure and/or wages rise to the ceiling (if there is one) is the most serious problem with the current severance payment system. Unlike the case of a defined contribution payment, employers cannot shift the liability to lower salaries. One of the clear effects of this mandate (Cox-Edwards 1996) is to make hiring decisions subject to the same delays that apply to investments in fixed assets, as indicated by evidence from Zimbabwe and India (Fallon and Lucas 1991), OECD countries (Lazear 1990), and Brazil (Anderson Schaffner 1993). The imputed cost of these mandated payments ranges from 5 to 12 percent of payroll wages with significant uncertainty, since most cases end up in court, compounding litigation and transaction fees. Small- and medium-size firms tend to be the most affected, and a single case can often lead them into bankruptcy (World Bank 1997a). Thus, their elimination (grandfathering the obligations and substituting them with an individual worker-capitalized fund, funded by employers' contributions of around 3 to 4 percent), would imply an employment increase of between 2 and 3 percent, incidence issues aside, given standard wage elasticities of employment.

In addition to the labor market barrier presented by the current structure of the severance system itself, having both a severance payment system and some form of unemployment insurance as some countries do (Argentina, Barbados, Brazil, Chile, Ecuador, and Venezuela) further aggravates labor market distortions. Their replacement with a fully funded severance payment system (defined contribution system) or other effective alternative needs to be considered. Some Latin American countries have already begun to transform their severance payment systems into some form of a deferred compensation scheme. Brazil, Trinidad and Tobago, and more recently Chile, Colombia, and Peru have replaced the traditional formula based on a month's pay times the number of years of service with a capitalized fund. Employers make a monthly contribution to a fund in the worker's name, portable to any job, accessible to the worker in the event of separation or retirement. For example, in Chile the PROTAC program (a labor training program) consists of the employer contributing monthly 3.6 percent of the worker's wages and the employee contributing 0.8 percent into a personalized account in his or her name in a financial institution. In the event of separation from the firm, the worker has access to the full amount in the account, plus the differential (to be contributed by the firm) that makes up a total compensation of one month per year of service, but with a maximum of eleven years. The total compensation is spread out over a maximum period of five months, which is the average unemployment duration in Chile.

This type of fund, a sort of savings account, is nondistortionary (as opposed to unemployment insurance) since it does not create disincentives for a worker to search for a job once unemployed or for a firm to hire additional workers, since the firm does not face any costs (certain or uncertain) when laying off workers. In addition, since the fund is, de facto, a deferred compensation, it should not translate into higher labor costs, but into lower nominal wages, except for workers being paid minimum wages (although not into lower total worker compensation). When workers secure other jobs, whatever unused amount is in the fund moves with them to their new jobs. On the other hand, the system is not fully efficient, since it does not pool risks across workers and does require individual contribution rates higher than optimal. Mixed systems can also be considered. Under a mixed system, for example, half of the mandated contribution goes to the individual worker's account, and the other half to a common fund. Two administrative options exist for a common fund: it could be administered (a) at the firm level by each individual firm or (b) at the economywide level by a government employment insurance entity. The common fund can then be used to complement individual funds in the event the latter lack sufficient money to offer minimum protection.

An additional benefit of reforming the severance payment regime is that, inasmuch as it reduces labor adjustment costs and uncertainty about them, it tends to reduce the level of informality in the economy, as demonstrated in Colombia (Lora and Henao 1995). (See box 7.1 for a discussion of the two salient approaches to providing support during unemployment.)

Box 7.1 Providing Support during Unemployment: Two Approaches

Nearly a full century has passed since the first formalized (but voluntary) unemployment insurance system was introduced in Belgium by small unions around 1900. Since then, all industrialized and many middle-income countries have introduced unemployment insurance systems. For countries such as Chile and Korea, which are considering introducing an unemployment insurance system, the experience of the industrialized countries can provide useful lessons.

Two types of unemployment support systems—defined as those providing support contingent upon voluntary separation from one's job—can be broadly distinguished.

• In one system, employers and/or employees contribute a certain fraction of wages and salaries to a common pool, which is used to pay benefits to eligible unemployed. This would be similar to a defined benefit pay-as-you-go pension system, with the difference that unemployment benefits are paid to those still active in the labor force. The U.S. system illustrates this "conventional" model.

• In the other system, employees and/or employers contribute toward an individual "contingency" fund, which is tapped when an individual (involuntarily) loses his or her job. In pension terminology, this would be an "individualized, capitalized, or fully funded" system. Brazil's *Fundo de Garantia por Tempo de Serviço* (FGTS), while not strictly an unemployment insurance system, perhaps best illustrates this system.

A. The U.S. Unemployment Insurance Fund

Most states in the United States do not mandate severance benefits. Workers whose contracts do not contain severance benefit clauses rely on personal savings and unemployment insurance while out of work.

Compulsory nationwide unemployment insurance was introduced as part of the Social Security Act of 1935. Following federal guidelines, all states have unemployment insurance systems. Those meeting Department of Labor approval receive federal transfers, funded through a federally mandated but state-administered tax on employers. The federal tax is 6.2 percent of the first $7,000 of each employee's earnings; employers in states conforming with federal standards receive a credit of 5.4 percent, yielding a net tax of 0.8 percent—a strong incentive for states to obey federal guidelines. States have the option of levying additional taxes for unemployment insurance, and 40 of them do (3 levy taxes on employees as well). States can "experience rate" the tax; that is, they can relate the rate to the frequency with which an employers' workers have claimed unemployment benefits. Most states replace 50 percent of a worker's lost wages for 26 weeks; the average benefit collection is 16 weeks.

In the U.S. system, between 80 and 90 percent of employees are covered. By all accounts, the U.S. system is well run, and the unemployment insurance fund is financially sound. But this does not rule out either disincentive effects or abuse of the system. Few dispute that its existence raises the unemployment rate: studies indicate that while the system does not increase the rate at which workers become unemployed (that is, incidence of unemployment), it does increase the duration of unemployment. Several states, such as Illinois, Kentucky, Massachusetts, New Jersey, and Pennsylvania, have experimented with incentives for early return to work. The abuse often takes place because of subjectivity in defining unemployment: while it is

(Box continues on the following page.)

relatively easy to tell if a person has lost his or her job, it is diffi-cult—even in an overwhelmingly formal labor market—to tell if he or she has found other work.

B. Brazil's Individualized Severance Funds

Unlike the United States, Brazil sought to provide some income sup-port during unemployment spells mainly by mandating severance benefits. In part this choice reflects the above-mentioned difficulty of determining whether a person is in fact out of work. Many develop-ing countries have also taken that route. Brazil's severance system is, however, quite unique. Since 1966, when hiring a worker, a firm has to deposit 8 percent of his or her wage in a special account—the *Fundo de Garantia por Tempo de Serviço*, or FGTS, account. In the case of justi-fied dismissal, workers can draw on their money during unemploy-ment. Initially, if fired "without just cause," workers would also receive 10 percent of the FGTS balance. In 1988 this amount was increased to 40 percent. In addition, the employer must notify workers one month before terminating employment, and allow them two hours a day to search for work.

In avoiding one problem, (that is, determining whether the per-son is in fact unemployed), the Brazilian system introduced many more problems (for example, litigation to decide whether the cause is "just" is creating a perverse incentive for workers to precipitate being fired in order to access the FGTS account balance, increasing observed turnover rates as a result). By one measure, the FGTS sys-tem design raises turnover rates in the Brazilian formal sector by as much as 30 percent, which is far above the normal turnover rate of 15–20 percent. Legislation designed to support workers during unemployment may also inadvertently lead to the belief that employment in Brazil's formal sector is "precarious" by in-ternational standards. In a more real sense, the higher turnover rates would lower firms' investments in workers' skills.

Since 1986, Brazilian workers have also been awarded the right to unemployment insurance, which initially offered partial coverage for up to four months of unemployment, and since 1966 has covered up to six months. This system is conventional, like that of the United States; however, it covers less than 25 percent of the country's labor force. But providing unemployment insurance when an adequate severance system is in place appears to be an overreaction and, over-all, the Brazilian system leads to excessive labor cost of separations.

Source: World Bank 1997b.

Decentralization of Collective Bargaining

Many LAC countries have a highly centralized collective bargaining system, particularly the larger countries—Argentina, Brazil, Uruguay, and Mexico. This provides a high degree of bargaining power and influence on market conditions to "representative unions," allowing them to negotiate conditions that apply both to their own enterprise and to the competition. Reforms can be implemented that would lower negotiation costs at all levels, removing the legally granted monopoly power over negotiations in the hands of sector unions. Decentralized bargaining obliges employers to bargain with plant-level unions, but does not preclude them from bargaining at a more centralized level, such as with industry-wide unions. The effect of decentralization would be a reduction in labor costs, with each firm adapting its compensation package to its own conditions, and an overall increased labor demand and greater economic activity. Wage flexibility is most necessary, particularly in noninflationary environments, which is the case in many LAC countries today. An additional advantage of this mode of reform is that, as opposed to lowering payroll taxes, it does not have an adverse fiscal effect.

As Heckman (1997) has eloquently pointed out, uniform regulations concerning wages and terms of employment applied crudely to unique situations distort productivity. Such restrictions do not capitalize on the local knowledge of participants, although a uniform set of rules facilitates transactions. Not only does mandated uniformity suppress the exploitation of the distinctive opportunities produced by the modern economy, but it also destroys the incentives for participants in diverse employment and production decisions to foster and use their knowledge. Industry-, sector-, or economywide bargaining rules in labor negotiations suppress the creation and use of situation-specific knowledge because parties are not free to act on what they know is good in any specific context, as do government regulations of the employment contract. Such regulations turn the attention of workers and firms toward the redistributive possibilities that flow from the application of uniform policies across broad sectors or the economy at large. Rent seeking, and not wealth creation, is a consequence of sectoral and national bargaining policies that favor some groups over others and draw government into setting wages. On the other hand, the evidence overwhelmingly indicates that when bargaining is takes place at the local level, wealth and jobs are created and unemployment declines.

Evidence and insight into the likely impact of opening the labor market to wage competition can be obtained through international comparisons and simulation models. The international evidence described below suggests the powerful impact of collective bargaining decentralization on job creation. Over a 15-year period, countries with decentralized systems outperformed countries with centralized systems on employment creation by more than 30 percent. In fact, for those countries with centralized collective bargaining, private employment declined slightly. In addition, Layard, Nickell, and Jackman (1991) analyzed the impact of the degree (the coverage rate) of centralized collective bargaining. Using cross-sectional analysis for 20 countries during 1983–88, they showed that the unemployment rate rises with collective bargaining's level of coverage; additional evidence is presented in appendix 2 and box 7.2.

Cox-Edwards (1996) provides results of simulations on the impact of the competitive opening of the labor market in Argentina.[14] Under specific assumptions on the values of basic parameters (which were calibrated to fit the starting conditions of the Argentine economy), this exercise suggests that a reduction of payroll taxes in the absence of industrial relations system reform can result in lower labor costs and more jobs, but may worsen the unemployment problem in the very short run, due to increased labor force participation. The reason: the tax reduction might allow an increase in real wages and in labor force participation in the short run, and thus might increase unemployment as a market-clearing mechanism. Simulating the effect of a change in the industrial relations system, which lowers inertia, points clearly to an equilibrium characterized by lower net wages and significantly lower unemployment rates and duration. The unemployment rate decreases by 4 percentage points. No reduction in unemployment appears until a reform in labor law eliminates inertia (statutory extensions of collective bargaining agreements at the sector level).

Box 7.2 Unionization Impact on Employment and Wages

As expected from wage determination mechanisms in the Caribbean, unionized sectors appear to earn higher wages than nonunionized sectors. For example, in Trinidad and Tobago, manufacturing sector workers in unionized firms earn over twice as much per hour as workers in small nonunionized firms for the same work. More generally, union wage premiums (estimated percentage difference between union and nonunion wages), tend to range from 10 to 30 percent (WDR 1995). In addition, a 1996 labor market study of Jamaica (Rama 1996) shows that the growth rate of employment is higher in firms where unionization is low. Employment is on average 4 percent lower in sectors where unionization is above average as compared to sectors where it is below average. Furthermore, differences exist in the way firms adjust to an expansion in economic activity. In sectors where firms are private and union membership is below average, the elasticity of employment to aggregate economic activity is about 3. But the elasticity falls to 1.2 in highly unionized sectors. Likewise, the elasticity of wages to economic activity is 1.1 in sectors with a low union presence, but 2.9 in sectors with a high union presence. Similarly, Panagides and Patrinos (1994), in a study of the impact of unions on wages in Mexico in the late 1980s, find a 10.4 percent union premium, after adjusting for differences in experience, education, sex, and sector. See also appendix 2.

Chapter 8
Evidence of the Impact of Labor Reforms

This chapter draws on international evidence for insight into the potential impact of reducing labor costs, eliminating inefficiencies, and making the labor market generally, and wage determination in particular, more competitive. It will first present the experience of those Latin American countries that have reformed their labor markets, and then will look at New Zealand's labor reform experience and the labor market structure of the East Asian countries. Finally, this chapter will compare U.S. and Western European labor market performance and examine more broadly the lessons from the OECD *Jobs Study 1994* on the impact of labor market structures on job creation.

The Impact on Employment of Labor Market Reforms: Latin America's Experience

Labor reforms in Chile, Colombia, and Peru made union representation contestable, extended the freedom to organize unions, and reduced the costs (or procedure-related uncertainties) of dismissals. All three countries reformed their labor codes to internalize the costs of labor disputes to the parties directly involved. In addition, Peru replaced the tradition of tripartite negotiations for "final offer" arbitration, eliminated job security laws, and reduced both the level and variance of severance payment packages for displaced workers.

Peru has seen significant growth in labor demand—on the order of 3.7 percent per year—and wage increases in the 1990s (see table 8.1). Using standard output elasticities, Peru's GDP growth can explain only 40 to 60 percent of labor demand increases. The remaining percentage can be attributed to labor reforms. Labor reforms in Chile took place in the context of broad, market-oriented reforms, the combination of which brought back dynamism in economic growth and employment creation. As figure 8.1 shows, employment has been growing steadily, and in particular, wage employment has seen a very sharp increase since the mid-1980s. While wage employment has grown at an average annual rate of 3.6 percent since 1977 and at 4.5 percent since 1984, the overall number of unionized workers has remained similar to that in the early

1970s, resulting in a unionization rate decline. Real wages rose 20 percent between 1989 and 1994, and strike activity has been substantially lower than in the premilitary period. Labor-related conflicts during 1988–91 are estimated at about 20 percent of the 1966–70 level (ILO 1994).

Since labor reform implementation, the export sectors have become very dynamic, leading those economies out of stagnation and unemployment (see tables 7.1, 7.2, and 8.1). Recent data from an employment survey in the greater Santiago area show that unemployment duration has fallen to 2.8 months, expected tenure has been steadily increasing, and the unemployment rate plummeted to 6 percent in 1996 (see table 8.2) and to 5.6 percent in the first quarter of 1997. While obviously not all the credit for the improvement in the employment outlook should be attributed to labor reforms, their contribution is nevertheless substantial. Again, the high Chilean GDP growth rates secured since the mid-1980s and the standard output-employment elasticities oscillating in the 0.55–0.25 range can explain only 40 to 60 percent of employment growth. In Colombia, labor reforms were enacted in 1990 affecting hiring conditions, severance payments, cost of dismissal, social security (reformed under a different law), minimum wages, and rules regulating collective bargaining. The employment scenario worsened in late 1996 and 1997, due mostly to a recession partly induced by political instability, an overvalued exchange rate, and some "Dutch Disease" symptoms.

What makes the Colombia case interesting is that in contrast to almost all other Latin American and Caribbean countries, it implemented its labor reforms very early in the transformation process—less than six months after the newly elected president took office. As a result, although unemployment reached an historic low of 8 percent in 1994, labor demand did not grow as much there as elsewhere. Further analysis reveals, however, a significant labor demand effect associated with labor reforms, and a structural change in the output/employment elasticity after the labor reforms. This effect did help labor market performance, although it was obscured in the aggregate figures because of a sharp increase in the capital output ratio between 1992 and 1994, associated with declining user costs of capital. "[H]ad the coefficients remained at their previous levels, labor demand would have been up to 28 percent smaller than it actually was" (Lora and Henao 1995, p. 15). In addition, Lora and Henao trace an important reduction in the degree of labor market informality between 1988 and 1994, and, based on their analysis, conclude that the reduction was the result of both the labor reforms and of a fall in the real level of the minimum wage. Overall, in all the countries mentioned in this chapter, unemployment fell within 12 months of enactment of labor reforms (see table 6.4).

Table 8.1 Evolution of Structure, Levels, and Growth of Urban Employment in Peru

	Percentage					People			Rate of Annual Growth		
	1990	1991	1992	1993	1994	1990	1992	1994	1990–92	1992–94	1990–94
Employed	91.7	94.1	80.6	90.1	91.2	2,330,875	2,471,709	2,685,932	3.0	4.2	3.6
Formal Sector	44.2	45.4	41.1	41.3	40.0	1,123,482	1,122,156	1,179,124	-0.1	2.5	1.2
Private	33.6	34.2	32.2	32.2	32.8	853,100	877,457	966,936	1.4	5.0	3.2
Public	10.6	11.2	9.0	9.1	7.2	270,381	244,699	212,189	-4.9	-6.9	-5.9
Informal Sector	42.8	44.2	45.0	44.7	47.0	1,088,518	1,228,439	1,383,255	6.2	6.1	6.2
Microenterprises[a]	10.5	11.4	11.2	13.3	14.9	265,720	306,492	437,807	7.4	19.5	13.3
Self-Employed[b]	32.4	32.8	33.8	31.4	32.1	822,799	821,947	945,448	5.9	1.3	3.5
Household Workers	4.7	4.5	4.4	4.1	4.2	118,875	121,114	123,553	0.9	1.0	1.0
Total Unemployment	8.3	5.9	9.4	9.9	8.8	210,973	256,447	259,169	10.3	0.5	5.3
Labor Force	100.0	100.0	100.0	100.0	100.0	2,541,848	2,728,155	2,945,101	3.6	3.9	3.7
Real Wage Index	195	224	216	214	248						
GDP Growth Rate	-3.8	2.9	-1.8	5.9	12.8						

Note: The data in this table refers to employment in metropolitan Lima.
a. Corresponds to establishments with five employees or less.
b. Includes self-employed workers and nonremunerated household workers.
Source: Yamada 1996.

The impact of decreased labor costs on labor demand can also be seen in Argentina's recent experience. From May 1996 to August 1997, 518,000 new jobs were created—the largest increase in 20 years. This turnaround is due to the combination of a 10 percent reduction in labor costs (real wages), the reform of the workers' compensation scheme (for job related accidents) that dropped the imputed cost from 4 percent to 1.5 percent of the wage bill, the use of flexible contracts, and a vigorous economic growth. The consequent increase in labor productivity, reflected in the decline of unitary labor costs of around 30 percent, has also effected a decline in Argentina's jobless rate, from 17.4 percent in October 1996 to 16.1 percent in May 1997 to 14 percent in October 1997 (*Informe de Coyuntura Laboral del MTSS* 1997). The overall impact and lag effect of economic liberalization and labor reforms on unemployment is shown in table 8.3.

Chilean labor reform made union representation contestable by establishing voluntary union affiliation even in enterprises with union representation, allowing more than one union to coexist in the same firm. This was a significant departure from the tradition of exclusive union representation given to a majority group. If voluntarily agreed to by workers' representatives and employers, negotiations could take place at the sector level between sectorwide unions and sectorwide employer representatives. Yet the reform eliminated the "duty to bargain" at any level above the enterprise. Employers were obliged to negotiate with enterprise unions only. Not surprisingly, the structure of worker representation has changed significantly since the reform, with clear reductions in the rate of unionization and average membership per union. Estimates for the greater Santiago area show that average hiring and firing rates increased from 20 to 30 percent per year after economic reforms, resulting in a net employment gain.

Figure 8.1 Employment Growth and Unionization in Chile

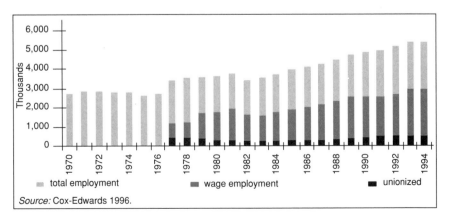

total employment   wage employment   unionized

Source: Cox-Edwards 1996.

Table 8.2 Chile: Labor Market Performance

Year	Expected Length of Unemployment (UE Duration)	Expected Permanency on the Job Tenure	Unemployment Rate
1982	10.2	34.0	22.1
1983	10.1	41.8	22.2
1984	7.8	41.8	19.2
1985	6.8	49.0	16.4
1986	4.9	39.6	13.5
1987	5.4	46.6	12.2
1988	4.0	41.5	10.9
1989	3.7	48.7	9.1
1990	3.3	38.2	9.6
1991	3.3	53.8	7.4
1992	3.0	56.6	6.0
1993	2.7	49.1	6.3
1994	2.8	49.1	6.8
1995	2.8	54.8	6.8

Source: Haindl, Gill, and Sapelli 1997, using Universidad de Chile surveys for the greater Santiago area.

Table 8.3 The Sequencing of Reforms and the Problem of Unemployment

Country	Stabilization	Timing of Reforms Trade Liberalization	Opening of the Formal Labor Market	Unemployment
Chile	1974–80	1976–80	1980–82	19% (1982)
Peru	1990–93	1990–93	1992–93	10% (1993)
Colombia	ongoing[a]	1990–92	1990	10% (1994)
New Zealand	1984–89	1985–93	1991	15% (1992)

a. Colombia has had annual inflation rates on the order of 30 percent for a long time. Stabilization efforts took that rate to about 20 percent in 1995.

Source: Cox-Edwards 1996.

The Chilean Case: A Closer Look at Inequality and Poverty

The Chilean case merits a closer look for two reasons. First, Chile is often looked upon as the example for Latin American countries to follow, and second, being the earliest reformer, it has an ample record of reforms' impacts, which allows for a sound evaluation. The Chilean case is also relevant since some have argued that labor market reforms that increase flexibility might have adverse impacts on earnings, inequality, and poverty. The focus here is on the impact of labor market reforms (but in the context of a broader set of reforms) on earnings, inequality, and poverty.

The Evolution and Reform of Labor Markets in Chile

Labor markets, their regulation, and institutions have changed profoundly during the last decades in Chile.[15] It is important to understand how the previous reforms were implemented in order to fully evaluate the potential of the present changes. This section provides a brief overview of what reforms have been made in Chile from 1973 to the present.

At first, as part of the policies of an authoritarian regime, the government tightly controlled the process of wage formation (1973–79). Then, as a consequence of external pressure, it authorized unionization and collective bargaining, but under restricted conditions (1979–89). Finally, with the restoration of democracy, the rules of the game changed again, so as to fully guarantee the rights to unionize and to bargain (from 1990 on).

A GOVERNMENT-CONTROLLED LABOR MARKET: 1973–79
For political reasons, the military government decided to ban a great number of unions and suspended collective bargaining and the right to strike. It replaced decentralized negotiations between firms and workers with a policy of wage readjustments determined by the authorities, made possible as a consequence of the extreme concentration of power in the military regime's hands. The incentives that conditioned the government's strategy stemmed either from economic circumstances or the internal politics of the regime, but not from a significant influence exerted by political parties or social sectors that opposed it.

Economic agents were unable to establish a significant degree of independence from official wage policies. So, to explain the evolution of real wages for this period, we must compare the official wage adjustment with the rate of change of the consumer price index (CPI). Given that wages were inflexible and did not accommodate diverse economic circumstances, employment followed the fate of aggregate demand during this period.

RESTRICTED LIBERALIZATION OF THE LABOR MARKET AND SOCIAL SECURITY REFORMS: 1979–89

By mid-1979 the Pinochet regime decided to legalize collective bargaining and eliminate a series of restrictions imposed on the labor movement. The boycott with which the international labor movement threatened Pinochet in late 1978 was the reason for this policy shift. Many aspects of labor laws were changed, including those concerning unions, collective bargaining, and individual contracts. Unilateral severance without stating cause and with no possibility of complaint was preserved, and severance payments were reduced to one month per year of service, with a five-year cap (allowing a maximum of five months' compensation).

The new legislation distinguished four different types of unions, and membership became voluntary. Unions were to be financed by membership dues. The regulations allowed collective bargaining only between an employer and one or more unions of the firm, or between the employer and groups of workers in the firm who organized specifically for collective bargaining purposes. Agreements reached were valid only for workers signing the agreement, and the minimum duration of a contract was set at two years, with no maximum.

The duration of a strike was limited to 60 days, after which job contracts expired automatically, with the worker losing the right to severance pay due to dismissal. Moreover, in 1982 mandatory indexation was eliminated for private-sector collective bargaining contracts, and public-sector wage increases ceased to be mandatory for private sector enterprises that were not negotiating collectively.

In 1981 the national pension system was changed from a government-run, pay-as-you-go arrangement to a privately managed contribution system. The new system basically consists of a mandatory savings program, managed by highly regulated private institutions, and a mechanism that, upon a worker's retirement, converts the fund accumulated in the savings accounts into indexed annuities. The use of individual accounts was supposed to make workers more conscious of the connection between their contributions and the pensions they would receive in the future. This would reduce the tax component of the pension contributions and, hence, reduce evasion and increase coverage. It would also favor employment creation. This effect, although conceptually correct, may not be as important as it seems if we take into account that (a) a significant number of workers will enjoy only the minimum pension guaranteed by the state; and (b) most workers, partly because of liquidity constraints, are subject to high rates of intertemporal substitution. The fact is that the system has not caused significant changes in the number of workers (as a portion of total employment) who contribute to the pension fund (Cortazar 1995). During this period wages grew at a fast pace—faster than the rate of productivity growth.

LABOR POLICY UNDER DEMOCRACY: 1990–97

The new government coalition—ranging from the political center to the left—emphasized the need for more equality and social participation in Chilean development. It also stressed the need to build a stronger social consensus in a society that had been highly polarized during the past decades. This strategy was called "growth with equality."

The government wanted to maintain a positive relationship with the labor movement (which required a decided will to introduce labor reforms), and a constructive relationship with business, as well as with the right-wing opposition that had a majority in the Senate and whose votes were necessary for any legal reform. In that context, five different labor policies were pursued: (a) social dialogue and tripartite agreements, (b) enactment of a new labor code, (c) improved enforcement of labor legislation, (d) implementation of a training program for young people, and (e) increased pensions and improvements to the national pension system. These reforms aimed to offset the unbalanced bargaining situation in which workers found themselves, without negatively affecting the flexibility and dynamism of the labor market.

The "needs of the firm" was reestablished as a cause for dismissal; inclusion of this cause afforded great flexibility to employers to alter their number of workers in crisis situations. The ceiling on service time applicable for severance payments was raised from 5 to 11 years for those workers hired after the reforms.

The same types of unions and voluntary membership were maintained. In addition, the law mandates that workers benefiting from the collective bargaining agreements must pay the negotiating union 75 percent of normal union dues for the duration of the contract, starting on the date on which the law's mandates apply to them; this attempts to correct the "free-rider" problem and improve the union's financial position. Collective bargaining can involve a single firm, or a group of firms when the parties voluntarily agree to that. That is a change from the previous law, which prohibited negotiation extending beyond the firm level. Only common working conditions, together with wages and other benefits, constitute matters of negotiation. Finally, two dispute-settlement mechanisms apart from striking are considered: mediation and arbitration.

Government intervention is significant at the policy level (tripartite national agreements, reform and enforcement of labor legislation, pensions, and resources for training), but not at the level of labor relations with the company, even in state enterprises' collective bargaining. However, while the legislation contained in the labor code is quite flexible, the legislation governing public sector workers is not; this hinders the task of modernizing the country's public sector, an indisputable requirement for more efficient and effective public policies.

Unemployment increased during the first year of the Aylwin government (1990–91) as a result of a restrictive macroeconomic policy aimed at decelerating inflation. Then gradually, over the next two years, unemployment began to drop as a consequence of the recovery in growth. Wages grew at an annual rate of almost 3.5 percent during that time. Five reasons lie behind these considerable wage rises: (a) high rates of productivity growth, (b) decelerating inflation (with relatively widespread indexation), (c) reductions in the unemployment rate, (d) generous increases in minimum wages and public sector wages, and (e) a better bargaining position for workers, thanks to the new legislation and the new social and political environment. The increase in unionization and collective bargaining occurred in the context of very little social unrest. During 1990–94, an average of one hour per worker was lost as a result of strikes and labor disputes. This is less than the average in OECD countries, and half the number recorded in Chile during the 1960s.

ISSUES REMAINING TO BE ADDRESSED
According to Mizala (1996) one of the persisting rigidities in the current law relates to severance payments. The argument used by the authorities in the Aylwin government for raising the maximum number of years' payment from 5 to 11 was the absence of alternative employment insurance to protect the unemployed worker, since the low level of existing unemployment compensation was considered insufficient. Discussion needs to resume on implementing a form of unemployment insurance that, while protecting workers in periods of unemployment, would also give greater flexibility to firms.

The need to bring more flexibility to labor regulation in the public sector should also be addressed, as the above comments suggest. Public services staffing and structure need to be brought in line with the new requirements generated by strengthening the state's regulatory function, primarily by improving the professional and technical level of those carrying out such functions.

The Evolution of Poverty and Income Distribution

Using a sample from the Encuesta de Caracterización Socioeconómica Nacional (CASEN), a nationally and regionally representative household survey conducted by the Ministerio de Planificación y Cooperación (MIDEPLAN) for the years 1987, 1990, 1992, and 1994, the World Bank (1997b) studied the evolution of poverty and income distribution in Chile during 1987–95.[16] Household survey data reveal unequivocally that Chile's growing economy and declining unemployment rate translated into real income gains, in terms of average labor earnings and of average per capita household and equivalent adult income levels, shown in figure 8.2.

Figure 8.2 Evolution of Poverty and Income Distribution in Chile

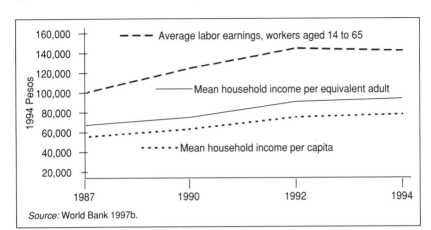

Source: World Bank 1997b.

Sustained GDP Growth, Declining Rates of Unemployment
As figure 6 indicates, GDP has been growing strongly in Chile for more than a decade, averaging more than 7 percent a year during 1985–95. This impressive growth record has been achieved mainly through a noninterventionist approach to markets and a liberalized trade regime. In the framework of flexible labor markets, unemployment in Chile has declined steadily over the same period, from a high of 17 percent in 1985 to about 6.6 percent in 1995, and real wages have consistently increased (see table 8.4).

The real income gains spawned by GDP and employment growth were shared among all income groups; average income rose for every decile over the period, with the bottom and top income earning groups experiencing the greatest increases (see figure 8.3).

Despite real increases over the entire period, average income and labor earnings figures reflect the economic slowdown that took place during 1992–94, when GDP growth declined from 11.8 percent in the second half of 1992 to 4.3 percent in 1994. Not surprisingly, the unemployment rate also increased in the same period from 4.9 to 6.3 percent.

WELFARE AND INCOME DISTRIBUTION
Social welfare increased and income inequality remained unchanged during 1985–95. Inequality, however, is fundamentally a measure of a distribution dispersion that is, by construction, insensitive to its mean. Sustained economic growth, which substantially raised the mean, ensured that social welfare was higher in 1994 than in 1987 by any reasonable measure, even though inequality remained unchanged. Similarly, poverty declined markedly from the beginning to the end of the period, and for a wide range of reasonable poverty lines.

**Figure 8.3 Annual Percentage Change of GDP and
Unemployment in Chile**

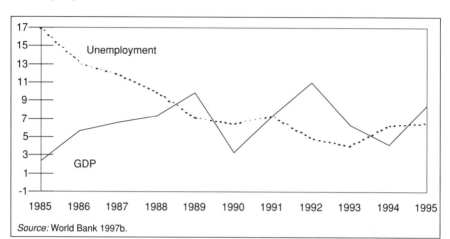

Source: World Bank 1997b.

While overall aggregate inequality was roughly constant, the shape of
the density function was changing slightly at the tails; there was some
compression at the bottom (particularly during the first three years of the
period), and some increased dispersion at the top. Moreover, the sustained
rise in mean decile income for all deciles reveals that the growth in mean
and median incomes did reach most Chileans (see figure 8.4).

**Figure 8.4 Percentage Change in Average Labor Earnings by
Income Decile in Chile**

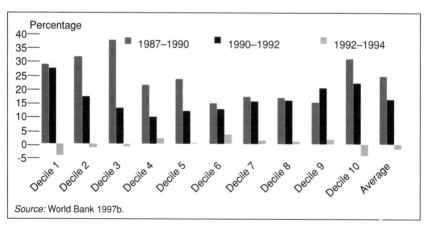

Source: World Bank 1997b.

In sum, although income shares of most deciles changed little over the period, for a wide range of eminently reasonable definitions of social welfare, including some of which are disproportionately sensitive to the welfare of the poorest members of society, welfare in Chile was unambiguously higher in 1991–92 than in previous sample years.

POVERTY
Poverty was without doubt lower in Chile in both 1992 and 1994 than in either 1987 or 1990. In this case, "without doubt" means that this poverty reduction would be registered by any poverty measure from a wide range of indices, such as head count and normalized poverty deficit, and with respect to any poverty line between P$15,050 and P$34,164. This strong result confirms that Chile has made substantial progress in poverty reduction during the last decade.

On the other hand, although indigence declined significantly between 1987 and 1992, it appears to have worsened between 1992 and 1994 (see figure 8.5). This follows directly from the income losses affecting the lowest decile and highlights the importance of detailed monitoring of living standards at a highly disaggregated level.

Figure 8.5 Measures of Wage Inequality for Full-time Male Workers in Chile

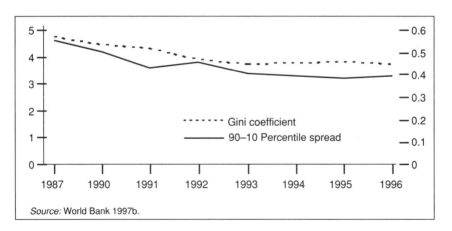

Source: World Bank 1997b.

Factors Behind Income Inequality
The World Bank analysis breaks down the mean log deviation of some of the inequality indices used into an explained component and a residual component. The explained component accounts for the effects of different

observables, such as gender, education, region, and age. Three main conclusions can be drawn.

1. A fine partitioning by six households or personal attributes[17] can account for more than half the total income inequality in Chile, a proportion that has remained remarkably stable over time. A relatively high proportion by international standards, it falls short of explaining the "causes" of inequality.

2. With the exception of education, individual partitions explain very little. At most, 10 percent of total inequality can be accounted for by differences among occupational categories. Regional differences account for 4 to 8 percent, and differences between households living in urban and rural areas account for marginally less. The unimportance of age and gender is surprising.

3. Education, measured as years of schooling, most powerfully explains inequality. Mean incomes rise in a pronounced manner with years of schooling, and inequality within each subgroup is generally much lower than the overall measure. It is very likely that the slight changes in inequality between 1987 and 1994 can be explained by changes in the differences between mean incomes accruing to different education subgroups.

Labor Markets, Inequality, and Poverty

MAIN FINDINGS

1. Between 1987 and 1992, average labor earnings increased by about 30 percent for the top and bottom quintiles, and by about 20 percent for the middle quintiles. Between 1992 and 1994, average earnings fell for the top and bottom groups, but rose modestly for the middle quintiles.

2. Wage inequality, as measured by the Gini coefficient and the spread between the 90th and the 10th percentile groups, rose between 1960 and 1987–88, but has declined significantly since then. This change in direction has been missed or underemphasized in many studies.

3. Rates of return to education behave in a similar way, rising from 1960 until 1987–88 and declining since then. Moreover, rates of return to education are lower for poorer groups.

4. The data contradict the widespread belief that employment and labor earnings are becoming more precarious. In the last decade, the labor market has become an increasingly reliable source of income: expected job tenure has increased, unemployment rates and duration have fallen, and long-term unemployment has become practically nonexistent.[18]

5. Simple simulations suggest that improved access to schooling by the poor will have relatively modest effects on earnings inequality, and this only at higher levels of education. Improvements in the quality of education appear to be much more effective than improvements in access to schooling.

Table 8.4 Evolution of the Share of Wages of Chile's GDP, 1987–93 (Percentage Annual Variation)

Year	(1) GDP	(2) Employment	(3) Average Productivity	(4) Real Wages	(5) Share of Remunerated Work in GDP
1987	6.6	3.5	3.1	–0.2	–3.3
1988	7.3	4.9	2.4	6.5	4.1
1989	9.9	5.2	4.7	1.9	–2.8
1990	3.3	2.0	1.3	1.8	0.5
1991	7.3	0.7	6.6	4.9	–1.7
1992	11.0	4.1	6.9	4.5	–2.4
1993	6.3	5.5	0.8	3.4[a]	2.6
1994	4.2	0.9	3.3	4.2[a]	0.9
1995	7.7[b]	1.1	6.6	4.2[a]	–2.4
Average 87–93	7.4	3.7	3.7	3.3	–0.4
Average 90–93	7.0	3.1	3.9	3.7	–0.2
Average 90–95	6.6	2.4	4.3	3.8	–0.5

(1) Annual variation in GDP.
(2) Annual variation in employment, yearly average.
(3) Rate of variation of average productivity = (1)–(2).
(4) Variation of real average wages (Instituto Nacional de Estadistica [INE]).
(5) Rate of change in the share of remunerations in GDP = (4)–(3).
a. Due to changes in methodology, figures for after 1993 are not comparable to pre-1973 series.
b. Average of first three quarters.
Source: Data for years 1987–93 is from Agacino (1994) cited in Leiva and Agacino (1994). Data for 1994 and 1995 and 1990–95 average, updated by author on the basis of INE.

Conclusions

Chile constitutes a model of economic reform for many LAC countries. From the evidence presented here, we can observe that the Chilean government's efforts to make the labor market more flexible, in the belief that this will eventually promote employment creation, and to simultaneously protect workers, have been enormous. They have paid off in terms of poverty reduction but, unfortunately, have not helped to measurably reduce income inequality. Moreover, we must remember that the prolonged period of intensive growth the Chilean economy has experienced in recent years (1987–94), and not these reforms alone, alleviated poverty. Therefore, we should conclude that, while employment creation is a main issue, so are inequality and poverty, and labor market reforms should be designed to address those two problems as well. Safety nets for the poor and the most exposed groups are necessary during the transition period, because most reforms will not immediately succeed.

The New Zealand Labor Market and Institutional Reform

New Zealand is an important case study in this context because of the systemic character of the labor reforms introduced by the Employment Act of 1991, designed to promote competitive behavior in the labor market. This act removed a long-standing bargaining obligation of employers: intended to make employment contracts similar to contracts in any other sphere of activity, it replaced centralized bargaining structures with decentralized enterprise bargaining. Under this act, employees freely choose their own bargaining agent, which can be themselves, a union, or any other agent (for example, a lawyer or labor relations specialist). The act gives no special status to unions, except to protect unions and union members from discrimination. No bargaining agent can bargain on behalf of any employee without written permission to do so.

Administrative extensions of collective contracts are a particularly potent mechanism by which to stifle competition in the labor market. When unions know their wages will be imposed on nonunion workers, an important restraint on wage demands—namely, the need to avoid pricing their members out of work—is removed. Moreover, incumbent firms may be more willing to yield to high-wage demands if they are sheltered from competing firms employing lower-wage workers. Abolition of administrative extensions would most likely result in a sharp reduction in the coverage of multiemployer collective contracts, since individual employers would have the freedom to attempt to gain a competitive edge in the product market by lowering labor costs. This is precisely what happened in New Zealand after the 1991 Employment Contracts Act (OECD 1994), with remarkable effects, at least from the employers' perspective. Union security law has been important, but closed shops are generally prohibited in Europe. The United Kingdom removed closed-shop arrangements in the 1980s; New Zealand eliminated all obligations of workers to belong to unions in 1991, and made compulsory membership illegal. The U.S. Supreme Court declared the preentry closed shop to be unconstitutional in the 1960s. Australia is one of the few countries were union security clauses are still used extensively.

As mentioned, New Zealand represents an important case study because of the systemic character of the labor reforms introduced by the 1991 employment act. In spite of sluggish economic growth in the 1980s, real wages had risen steadily from 1984 to 1988. A broad economic reform program , implemented in the late 1980s, had lowered inflation from a moderate rate and liberalized trade. Unemployment started to rise in 1987 and accelerated again in 1990, climbing above 10 percent. The effects of tight monetary control and the restructuring induced by increasing competition in the products market produced significant job losses. The economy needed an increased labor demand to add dynamism to job creation.

New Zealand's experience has some commonalties with that of Chile. Although Chile started from a much more distorted position (600 percent inflation, and much higher effective rates of protection), in both countries stabilization was followed closely by trade liberalization, and domestic markets and labor reforms took some time. In both countries the real exchange rates went out of line, indicating that the economies were unable to compete in the export market. After labor reforms, the export sectors have become very dynamic, leading these two economies out of stagnation and high unemployment. These two cases contrast sharply with the experiences of Colombia and Peru, where labor market reforms were implemented earlier, improving the real exchange rate position and maintaining the unemployment rate at a moderate level.

Figure 8.6 summarizes survey results from a sample of 673 New Zealand enterprises in 1993, which were asked to evaluate their business situation relative to what they thought it would have been in the absence of the labor reform. Their assessment indicates that reforms improved incentives to create jobs by increasing operational flexibility, labor productivity, and management quality, and by reducing hiring and firing costs.

Figure 8.6 The Impact of New Zealand's 1993 Labor Reform

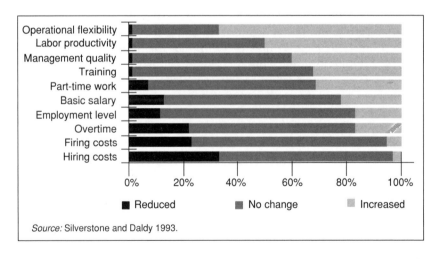

Source: Silverstone and Daldy 1993.

The United States vs. European Union Labor Market Models: A Performance Comparison of Flexible vs. Rigid Labor Market Models

To further illustrate the consequences on employment of pursuing alternative patterns of labor reform, a comparison can be made between two salient approaches to labor market policies in the developed world—low labor costs versus high labor costs.[19] The U.S.-type of labor market policies emphasizes fully flexible labor markets with basic welfare protection, contractual freedom, low cost of labor adjustments, and decentralized collective bargaining. Then there is the European Union (EU) labor market approach, based on generous benefits and welfare protection (financed by high non-wage labor costs), high levels of job security, reduced contractual freedom, and highly centralized collective bargaining. The strikingly different employment performance over the last decades between the two types has been extensively studied (Siebert 1997; Nickell 1982, 1997), with differences largely attributed to the significantly higher level of welfare benefits for the unemployed, and to the EU countries' higher levels of protection and rigidities.

Cost of Labor Adjustment in the EU. The average cost of firing a worker in the EU is 22 weeks' wages (26 for white-collar workers and 16 for blue-collar workers), and most countries require statutory consultations with unions or the state. Denmark, Ireland, and the United Kingdom have the fewest restrictions; Greece, Italy, Portugal, Spain, and the Netherlands have the most; Belgium, France, and Germany lie in between the two extremes. Many southern European countries, with their low work-force participation rates and high long-term unemployment, illustrate the point that the more regulations protect full-time jobs, the fewer jobs employers will offer. In Spain and Italy, it can cost more than two years' pay to fire a worker.[20] Restrictions on temporary work have resulted in only 9 percent of EU workers being temporary.

Unemployment in the EU. In OECD countries between 1979 and 1994, unemployment rose from 17.7 million and a rate of 5.1 percent, to 34 million and a rate of 8 percent. In EU countries, the unemployment numbers are particularly worrisome, reaching historical highs in most countries. The EU countries lost a net of 6 million jobs between 1990 and 1996, and have the same number of jobs as in 1980. Since 1970 the number of private-sector jobs has shrunk by 3 million. The unemployment rate in France during the 1960s and early 1970s was 2.6 percent; since the early 1990s it has been gradually increasing, reaching 12.8 percent in 1997. Germany's unemployment rate was below 1 percent in previous decades but reached 11.2 percent in 1997. In Italy, the unemployment rate reached 12.1 percent in 1997; in Canada, 9.6 percent; in Spain, 21.8 percent. In Belgium the unemployment rate has quadrupled over the past 20 years, reaching 13.1 percent in 1997. Sweden's unemployment rate reached 10.9 percent in 1997 (see table 8.5).

Table 8.5 Unemployment in the European Union

	Total			Women			Youths (less than 25 years)		
	1996	1997	Feb. 1998	1996	1997	Feb. 1998	1996	1997	Feb. 1998
Austria	4.4	4.3	4.4	5.2	3.5	3.6	6.1	6.7	6.6
Belgium	11.0	13.1	12.3	13.1	9.3	9.0	23.4	23.0	22.3
Denmark	7.2	6.4	5.5	8.7	5.1	4.1	11.5	8.9	7.0
Finland	15.6	15.1	12.5	15.5	14.1	11.5	28.7	29.1	25.7
France	12.3	12.8	12.1	14.5	10.7	10.3	28.5	29.4	27.2
Germany	9.4	11.2	11.4	9.8	10.2	10.8	9.9	11.8	11.4
Ireland	12.0	10.6	9.6	12.3	10.5	9.4	18.8	16.8	14.3
Italy	12.0	12.1	—	16.3	9.5	—	33.3	33.4	—
Luxembourg	3.1	3.6	3.4	4.5	2.8	2.3	8.9	9.8	7.9
Netherlands	6.4	5.6	—	8.1	4.4	—	11.3	9.9	—
Portugal	7.3	7.2	6.6	8.1	6.4	5.7	16.6	16.2	15.2
Spain	22.7	21.8	20.0	29.9	16.6	15.1	42.7	40.0	37.0
Sweden	9.6	10.9	9.0	9.2	11.3	9.2	20.8	22.1	18.0
United Kingdom	8.4	7.3	6.6	6.5	8.3	7.0	15.5	14.8	12.6
EU	11.2	12.3	11.4	12.5	11.4	9.9	21.9	21.5	20.0

Source: Eurostat and individual country reports. Data unavailable for Greece.

French and German interventionist policies maintain wage levels and social safety nets at the cost of higher unemployment; high tax rates are also stifling business development. Even Japan, which used to have negligible unemployment rates, reached 3.4 percent in 1996. Only the United Kingdom has shown improvement among these OECD countries, with robust employment growth and a reduction of the unemployment rate to 6.6 percent in 1998, a seven-year low. The United Kingdom has the most flexible labor market (the product of former Prime Minister Margaret Thatcher's reforms) among the EU countries, which to a large extent explains its differential employment performance. In all, there are now 22 million unemployed workers in the Group of Seven (G-7) countries, and most of them are long-term unemployed. In the European Union, more than 50 percent of the unemployed have been without a job for over a year (see table 8.6). While some level of unemployment is desirable, long-term unemployment is not. The incidence of high long-term unemployment and rising levels of unemployment clearly indicate labor market failures.

Unemployment/employment in the United States. While the EU has lost 6 million jobs between 1990 and 1996, the United States has gained 12.6 million jobs. As of January 1999, the latter reached a 28-year low in unemployment, with a rate of 4.3 percent, and has enjoyed unemployment rates below 7 percent during the 1990s. The U.S. economy created 8.5 million new jobs in a 3-year period (1993–96). In addition, in 1980, U.S. employment grew by nearly 35 percent, while most of the EU countries barely maintained 1980 employment levels (see figure 8.7 and table 8.7). In summation, for the last 30 years the United States has shown significant employment and job creation growth, while EU employment growth has been stagnant for most of its member countries. Further contrasting with the EU is the number of the long-term unemployed: in the U.S. only 5.6 percent of the jobless are long-term unemployed. The difference between the numbers is even more striking, considering that the growth of the U.S. labor force has been significantly higher than that of the EU. While the population, labor force, and labor force participation in the United States have been growing by more than 1 percent per year, in the EU, growth has been on the order of 0.2 percent per year. In addition, labor force participation is also considerably higher in the United States, compared to the EU (77.8 percent vs. 67.5 percent, respectively, as of 1996; see table 8.6 below).

Table 8.6 United States vs. European Union Labor Market Performance

	United States	European Union
Net jobs created 1990–96	12.5 million	–6 million
Net private sector jobs created 1970–96	44 million	3 million
Average annual employment growth 1980-98	1.6%	0.3%
Unemployment rate 1997 (April 1998)	4.9% (4.3%)	12.1%
Incidence of long-term unemployment	5.6%	53%
Real earnings growth 1976–96	2%	25%
Average annual return on equity 1974–94	9%	7%
Average annual labor productivity growth 1979–95	0.85%	1.8%
Labor force participation 1995	77.8%	67.5%
Labor force 1995	131 million	164 million
Annual growth of labor force 1980–95	1%	0.2%

Source: Author compilation based on U.S. Bureau of Labor Statistics and OECD data.

**Figure 8.7 Employment Creation in the US and the EU
Estimated change, 1970–94 (in millions)**

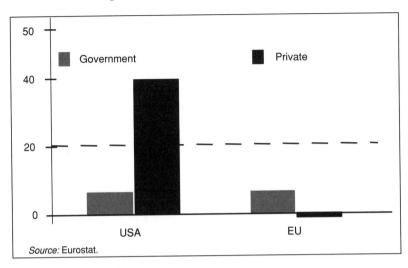

Source: Eurostat.

Table 8.7 OECD: Employment Effects of Changes in Payroll Tax Rates

Country Study	Result
UK-a (1986)	13 percentage point rise in taxes increases unemployment by 1.4 percentage points.
UK-b (1987)	Increase in payroll taxes increased real wages in the short term, so likely reduced employment immediately.
UK-c (1993)	Increase in payroll taxes led to increase in unemployment.
Canada (1990)	Payroll taxes have increased structural unemployment by 2.5 percentage points.
Denmark (1990)	Increase in payroll taxes increased real wages by the same amount, implying a fall in employment.
Norway (1990, 1988, 1989)	10% increase in payroll taxes increased wages between 8–10%, implying a fall in employment.
Denmark and Norway (1990)	Increase in payroll taxes increased real wages in the short term only; no long term effect on employment.
Finland (1990)	Small long-term impact on wages and employment.
Finland and Norway (1985)	Increase in payroll taxes increased real wages in the short term only; on long term effect on employment.
Italy (1990)	Increase in payroll taxes led to increase in unemployment.
Spain (1986)	Significant effect on real wages and thus reduced employment.
OECD-a (1986)	Increase in payroll taxes responsible for about 50% of the increase in unemployment.
OECD-b (1991)	Significant effect on real wages, and so reduced employment.

Source: OECD Employment Outlook (1998)

Earnings in the United States vs. the European Union. Major job creation has come at the cost of lower earnings growth in the United States, particularly for unskilled workers. Real earnings in the EU have increased significantly, while there has been a much lower increase in the United States. At the bottom decile of the U.S. earnings distribution, real earnings have decreased by over 10 percent for men and about 3 percent for women during 1985–95. Men and women in the top decile have seen their earnings grow by about 4 percent and 16 percent, respectively, over the same period. While pinpointing the factors that have contributed to growing wage dispersion in the United States is difficult, the most compelling explanation is that technological advances have increased highly trained workers' productivity more than that of less-skilled workers. Over the last 10 to 15 years, the supply of highly educated U.S. workers has simply not kept pace with the steadily increasing demand. It may be too soon to tell where the trend toward increased income dispersion in the United States is headed. Moreover, individual earnings are only a part of the household well-being equation. The *1997 Economic Report of the President* found, in fact, that between 1993 and 1995, income grew among households at every income level, with the greatest increases (3.5 percent) registering among families in the bottom quintile of income distribution.

At the low end of the U.S. earnings distribution, real earnings (minimum wages) have decreased by 11 percent since 1972, while at the top, they have increased by 4.4 percent. However, these figures are based on the earnings of full-time male and female workers, separately compiled. In the United States, male–female average wage differentials have narrowed, and when all earners are included, real earnings at the bottom decile have increased. Clearly, considering only full-time earners (about 70 percent of all earners) makes a big difference . But considering all earners, pooling of their earnings into household earnings, and questioning earners' mobility are important to assess U.S. labor market developments from an equity standpoint. In the United States, nearly half of the displaced, formerly full-time wage and salaried workers report increased earnings in their new jobs, and only 8 percent of the displaced workers end up in part-time jobs. Nearly 60 percent of dismissed workers who find jobs after a layoff do so only at lower levels of pay, and most of those workers are still earning much less even five years later. This trend holds across all levels of schooling. On income distribution, flexible markets tend to produce wider disparities, as figure 8.8 shows. The United States and Canada lead the gap differential between the after-tax earnings of the 10 percent poorest families of four and the 10 percent richest families of four, although to some extent the wider differential in those countries reflects their wider distribution of skills and productivity, measured by schooling years.

A comparison of these two types of labor markets and institutions appears to favor (in terms of efficiency and welfare) the U.S. type of labor market. Its benefits significantly outweigh its losses when compared to the EU type.

Job Tenure in the United States vs. the European Union. The flexibility of the U.S. labor market has led to stronger job creation, lower unemployment rates, and shorter unemployment spells. The possibly negative aspects of such labor market flexibility may be less real earnings growth and less job security, and the effect that higher turnover rates may have on the quality of the labor force (for example, training). The relationships among labor market flexibility, turnover rates, training, and labor force quality are debatable, however. The evidence suggests that in the more flexible U.S. labor market environment, workers on average spend fewer years with a single employer (that is, job tenure is lower) than do their European counterparts, although the difference varies by country (see table 8.8). The average tenure of workers in Australia, Britain, Canada, and the Netherlands, for example, is close to the U.S. figure of 6.7 years, while France, Germany, Italy, and Spain have numbers closer to the average tenure of employees in Japan: 10.9 years.

Table 8.8 Average Tenure—Years of Workers with Same Current Employer, as of 1994

United States	6.7
Australia	6.8
Holland	7.0
Canada	7.8
Britain	7.9
Switzerland	8.8
Spain	9.8
France	10.1
Germany	10.4
Italy	10.5
Japan	10.9

Source: OECD Jobs Study 1994.

The difference in average tenure is greatest between the United States and Japan. In Japan, 10 percent of all workers have been at their current job less than a year and 37 percent for less than five years, whereas the U.S. figures are 29 percent and 62 percent, respectively. The current tenure-years figure does not predict how long employees *will* stay with their current employers, although it does reflect greater turnover in the United States, relative to Japan. In fact, only 25 percent of Americans stay at their jobs for more than 10 years, while 40 percent of Japanese do so.

Training. One potentially negative effect of a more flexible labor market, in which firms face lower costs of hiring and shedding labor, is the impact that fewer average tenure-years may have on the willingness of firms to train their employees. Indeed, only 10 percent of U.S. recruits receive formal training, compared with 70 percent of Japanese and German workers. While employers may have fewer incentives to train workers who switch jobs more frequently, however, those employees may face greater incentives to acquire skills training on their own, based on the perceived demand for those skills in the labor market. Moreover, higher turnover rates may reflect better matching between employers and employees, given the lower costs to firms of hiring and shedding labor as needed.

Added Deregulation Benefits. Finally, further evidence of the adverse impact of rigid labor markets comes from a number of studies analyzing the annual GDP benefits of broad economic regulatory reform. Most of these studies show that the benefits double when labor markets are flexible. For example, in the Netherlands the annual GDP benefits of regulatory reform were estimated at 0.5 percent, and even, provided labor markets were flexible, at 1.1 percent (Westerhout and van Sinderen 1994).

Reasons Behind EU and U.S. Differential Employment Performance. Clearly the significant employment performance differences between the markets in the U.S. and European Union are not due to insufficient demand, growth, or investment in Europe, as is often argued. As illustrated in figure 8.8, real GDP growth has been the same in both the United States and the EU, and the capital stock has actually grown slightly faster in the latter than in the former. Thus, the unemployment differences cannot be attributed to those two factors. Some have argued that the worsening has been due to the austerity measures implemented by some EU countries to comply with the Maastricht Treaty, which established the European Monetary Union. While that has obviously not helped the outlook, the differential performance existed for some time before those measures were considered. Where a difference indeed does exist is in the labor market structure; hence, a salient explanation, based on differential labor costs (rigidities) and capital/labor relative costs, cannot be rejected.[21]

Not surprisingly, a difference exists in the capital–labor ratio in the United States and the EU, illustrated in figure 8.8. In Europe, the amount of capital per worker has been rising sharply, indicating capital deepening, or a substitution of capital for labor. In contrast, the lower increase in the U.S. capital–labor ratio suggests capital widening, or the expansion of capacity. This difference is consistent with, and most likely is induced by, the different flexibility of labor market structures. While 'he United States, with a much more flexible structure, encourages employment growth, the EU does not. Rapid real wage growth in Europe has encouraged capital–labor substitution, while that has not been the case in the United States, given its tepid wage growth. A further difference affecting employment growth is the frequent increases in wages outpacing increases in productivity in EU countries, while the opposite is the case in the United States, as shown in table 8.9. The pay of EU workers rose above productivity growth by nearly 3 percent per year in real terms during the 1980s, while it stayed the same in both the United States and Japan.

Centralized collective bargaining was in part responsible for that growth (at the expense of employment growth). As long as productivity increases are fully absorbed in wage increases, no increases in competitiveness or reductions in labor costs take place, and employment growth is thus hampered. Nickell (1997), in a comprehensive econometric study of the issue, reported that the higher unemployment of the EU is associated with (a) generous unemployment benefits that are allowed to run on indefinitely, combined with little or no pressure to obtain work and low levels of active intervention to increase the ability or unwillingness of the unemployed to find work; (b) high unionization with wages bargained collectively and centralized, and no coordination between unions and employers in wage bargaining; (c) high overall taxes impinging on labor, or a combination of high minimum wages for young people associated with high payroll taxes; and (d) poor educational standards at the bottom of the labor market. Similarly, Siebert (1997) found that the institutional labor market differences between Europe and the United States can explain their different employment pictures. Overall, the theory and evidence quite unambiguously indicate that the strikingly different employment performance of the United States and the EU can by and large be attributed to their different labor market structures and associated benefits.

Labor Reform in Europe: Different Alternatives
The rapid deterioration of the employment outlook in EU countries has led to a search for alternatives to labor reform. The process has proven to be difficult since it involves the relinquishing of highly valuable (yet costly and less and less sustainable) acquired rights and benefits. Successful reforms are feasible, as the U.K. case illustrates. To date, the reform experiences of other countries have been mixed, with the Netherlands case being an interesting and promising one, illustrating the possibilities.

Figure 8.8 United States vs. European Union: GDP, Investment, and Capital-Labor Ratio Performance

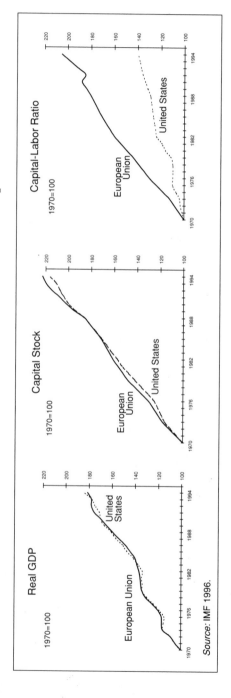

Source: IMF 1996.

The Netherlands Case. Currently, unemployment in the Netherlands is only 6.2 percent, half of what it was in 1983. The most interesting characteristics of the reform are the fact that is was almost conflict-free and that it did not sacrifice the national goal of redistribution from the rich to the poor. For those reasons, the Netherlands reform model might seem quite appealing to other countries in the EU that view U.S.-like measures as too extreme, or that are concerned about the possible impact on inequality.

The main features of the Netherlands' labor market reform are summarized in box 8.1. Although it is true that the Dutch performance has not been extraordinary (unemployment is low, but so is employment growth; many people seem to have dropped out of the labor force), its achievements are definitely better than those of other EU economies.

Table 8.9 Wage and Productivity Increases, 1994–95 (Percentage)

Country	A. Productivity (output/hour)	B. Hourly Wage	C. Net Productivity Gain (A-B)
United States	3.4	2.8	0.6
Canada	1.6	1.2	0.4
Japan	5.4	3.2	2.2
Germany	3.2	5.1	-1.9
Sweden	3.4	5.4	-2

Source: U.S. Department of Labor, Bureau of Labor Statistics 1996.

Other Countries. There have been other attempts to reform, with arguably mixed results. As described, the most successful reform in terms of employment growth has been in the United Kingdom, where U.S.-type system reforms to make labor markets flexible (that is, to reduce costs) were undertaken during the 1980s. France considered but failed to implement a reduction in social benefits, due to massive protests and pressure from workers. France is also considering a reduction in the work week as an incentive to work sharing, but this measure could very easily reduce productivity as well. Some years ago, Spain introduced part-time contracts that offer less job protection, and about 30 percent of the workers are employed under such conditions. However, those new contractual forms' effect on net employment creation has been, at most, minor. For the most part, senior workers have been replaced by younger workers and women, and a dual labor force has been created—that is, a labor force with employed workers in the formal sector who are highly protected, and another composed of part-timers or those on temporary contracts who are extremely unprotected and have high labor turnover rates.

Box 8.1 Labor Market Reform in the Netherlands

Public spending cuts from 60 percent to 50 percent of GDP

Reduction of employers' social security contributions from almost 20 percent to only 7.9 percent

Reduction of the bottom rate of income tax from 14 percent to 7 percent, while top marginal rates remained at 60 percent

Part-time work made easier by permitting part-timers to be paid less than full-timers for the same job

Centralized wage bargaining helped to build a consensus in favor of wage restraint

Unemployment insurance and disability insurance cut from 80 percent to 70 percent of final pay

---

The Political Issue. The main explanation for why many EU countries have failed to implement more radical reforms lies in European politics and can be described in terms of the outsider–insider model. Laws designed to protect workers raise the cost of firing employees and make companies less willing to take the risk of creating jobs. But if the laws damage the economy as a whole, they benefit one important group: those already employed. The laws help them by making their jobs more secure and by enabling them to bargain for higher wages without fear of redundancy (*The Economist* 1997). Saint-Paul (1996) finds that across-the-board reforms tend to be implemented under right-wing governments, just as targeted increases in protection are associated with left-wing parties. In addition, under both types of government, partial freeing up of the labor market tends to happen when unemployment is increasing. In contrast, general increases in protection occur when unemployment is falling and growth is above average (that is, when workers demand a share of prosperity from their employers).

Prospects in the EU. While the European labor welfare system appeared sustainable under the old economic order of relatively closed and protected economies and moderate growth, it has begun to unravel under the competitive pressures induced by ever-increasing openness and globalization of economies, and lower growth. The high cost brought about by a protected labor market system and generous benefits is undermining productivity and competitiveness in the EU vis-à-vis lower-cost countries. Not surprisingly, the lower productivity and lower growth experienced in the developed world during the last decades has created strains in the labor market and shown the employment impact of different labor policies. Productivity in the United States averaged 1.1 percent annually during 1973–94, while it was 3 percent during 1960–73. In the EU, productivity growth was 1.7 percent during 1973–94, and 2.5 percent in Japan. GDP growth in most of those countries averaged 3.5 percent in 1960s, and in the 1990s has declined to 2.1 percent per year. Without labor reforms, the employment numbers in the EU are likely to worsen. Under globalization, the current structure is not in equilibrium, and thus is not sustainable. High labor costs, induced by high labor taxes and high real growth, lead to reduced competitiveness, loss of market share by EU firms, the transfer of productive activities to low labor cost countries, and to increased substitution of labor for capital—all with obvious adverse effects on job creation. The lessons for developing countries are clear, and the choice is theirs.

The East Asia Experience

Comparing the job creation performance of East Asia and LAC is also of interest, since the severity of LAC's labor market regulations contrasts sharply with the extreme flexibility of the East Asian countries. A proxy for degree of regulation is the number of ILO conventions ratified by countries as of October 1994: in East Asia—Hong Kong (0), Indonesia (10), Korea (4), Malaysia (11), Singapore (21), and Thailand (11); in LAC—Argentina (67), Brazil (76), Colombia (52), Ecuador (56), Guatemala (67), Mexico (76), Nicaragua (58), Peru (67), Uruguay (97), and Venezuela (52). For comparison purposes, the number in other countries is France (115), Germany (75), Italy (102), Spain (124), the Netherlands (94), and the United States (11).[22] The economic performance of most East Asian countries since the 1970s was spectacular until stopped by the 1997 financial crisis in that region. From the 1970s until 1997, most East Asian countries experienced robust employment growth (1.5 to 3 percent), real wage growth (4 to 6 percent), and very low unemployment rates (3 to 8 percent) in an environment of high GDP growth (5 to 8 percent).

   A relatively high level of efficiency in labor allocation was achieved by allowing wages and employment to be determined by and large by the interaction of those supplying and those demanding labor services, rather than by government legislation, public-sector leadership, or union pressure. Wages were pulled up by increases in the demand for labor, rather than being pushed up artificially; earnings growth was determined more by the growth of the economy as a whole than by the growth in any particular sector (Fields 1992). A number of East Asian countries intervened in labor markets to suppress the activities of industry- or economywide unions and to ensure that wage agreements were set at the enterprise level. The flexible labor markets allowed wages to be responsive to changes in the demand for labor and, as a result, adjustments to external macroeconomics shocks, such as those induced by the oil crisis of the 1970s, were often quicker and less painful in these East Asian countries (Mazumdar 1993). While a plethora of factors contributed to that excellent performance, the labor market conditions in those East Asian countries was indeed one of the major factors, as is shown and argued in *The East Asian Miracle* (World Bank 1993). Yet this does not mean that the East Asian labor market model is to be imitated in toto, since it does suffer from basic problems, such as the abuse of child labor, minimum worker rights, and weak social protection.

Lessons of the Impact of Labor Market Structure on Employment Creation from the *OECD Jobs Study*

The OECD *Jobs Study 1994* provides further evidence on the employment impact of job protection measures, centralized collective bargaining, and the impact of labor costs (OECD *Jobs Study 1994*, Part II).

(a) *Job Protection Measures.* A clear relationship exists between the number of employment protection laws and job turnover, and consequently between employment protection laws and long-term unemployment (Nickell 1982). The *OECD Jobs Study* also shows a strong and significant correlation between various employment and self-employment ratios and various measures and indexes of the strength of job protection. Most measures of the employment/population ratio in 1990 tend to be lower in countries with high levels of employment security. Self-employment and non-agricultural self-employment tend to be higher in countries that have strict protection. In a 1989 European Community survey, for example, well over half of the firms surveyed in countries with relatively strict employment protection reported that hiring and firing procedures and associated costs were one reason for not hiring more workers. This was not the case for firms in countries with fewer restrictions on employee dismissal.

(b) *Centralized Collective Bargaining.* The OECD *Jobs Study* also examined how the degree of centralization of collective bargaining correlated with employment growth between 1973 and 1989. For this purpose, countries were classified in terms of (a) bargaining levels as centralized, sectoral, and company–plant, and (b) bargaining coordination as high, low, and none (see table 8.10). The study found a much more robust employment growth in the private sector—30 percent higher—in countries with decentralized (company–plant) bargaining. Any employment growth over the period in the centralized countries occurred in the public sector. The results did not depend on the initial employment conditions, since both sets of countries had similar employment–unemployment rates. The 30 percent differential in private-sector employment in the decentralized countries is at least suggestive of the impact that decentralization of collective bargaining could have in those LAC countries that still have centralized collective bargaining.

(c) *Impact of Labor Cost.* International experience confirms the importance of labor costs in the employment picture. Private job creation in the 1980s and 1990s has been fastest in countries where the relative wage of lower-skilled workers has fallen the most. Thus, Australia, Canada, Japan, and the United States have all seen solid gains in private sector employment at a time when their earnings distribution was widening. In the United Kingdom in particular, the sharp decrease in the relative wage of low-productivity workers in the latter part of the 1980s is likely to have contributed to the strong gains in private-sector employment. Institutional constraints on wages at the lower end can prevent wages from being aligned with productivity levels and can increase the danger that some workers are barred from employment anywhere in the economy because of wages in excess of expected productivity.[23]

Table 8.10 Bargaining Levels, Bargaining Coordination, and Labor Market Performance

	Level in 1989 (1973 = 100)		
Classification (1)	Total Employment	*Private Employment*	Public Employment
Bargaining Levels (2)			
Centralized	111	**99**	160
Sectoral	109	**105**	137
Company–plant	129	**130**	127
Bargaining Coordination (3)			
High	115	114	128
Low	106	101	145
Zero	133	135	128

(1) Classification based on bargaining arrangements in the 1970s.

(2) *Centralized*: Austria, Denmark, Finland, Norway, Sweden; *sectoral*: Australia, Belgium, France, Germany, Italy, the Netherlands, New Zealand, Portugal, Spain, Switzerland; *company*: Canada, Japan, United Kingdom, United States.

(3) *High*: Australia, Germany, Japan; *low*: Belgium, Denmark, Finland, France, the Netherlands, Norway, Portugal, Spain, Sweden, Switzerland; *zero*: Canada, New Zealand, United Kingdom, United States.

Source: OECD *Jobs Study 1994, Part II*, table 5.15, p.19.

Substantial evidence exists that demand for labor is negatively related to labor costs in the long run, particularly in the economy's market sector. Empirical labor demand equations suggest that long-run reactions of private-sector employment to changes in labor costs are similar across countries, but point up striking differences between countries in terms of how quickly labor demand responds (Hamermesh 1993; Jarret and Torres 1987; Turner, Richardson, and Rauffet 1993). OECD estimates suggest that a 1 percent reduction in labor costs typically increases labor demand in the pri-

vate sector by 1 percent; that is, the wage-employment elasticity is close to
–1 (see table 8.11). However, countries differ in the speed of adjustment.
The United States and Canada, where the lock-in of wage contracts is weak-
est and the labor markets are most flexible, are, not surprisingly, the countries with the fastest adjustments.

Table 8.11 Selected Wage Elasticities and Median Log Response

	Wage-Employment Elasticity	Median Lag (Years)
Argentina	–0.5	3.0
United States	–1.0	1.0
Japan	–0.8	3.0
Germany	–1.0	2.0
France	–1.0	2.0
Italy	–0.5	5.0
United Kingdom	–1.0	4.0
Canada	–0.5	1.0
Australia	–1.0	2.0
Sweden	–0.9	7.0
Finland	–1.0	3.0

Source: Tyrvainen 1996; Guasch, Gill, and Pessino 1996.

Chapter 9

Public Policy Implications

In designing public policy in labor markets, compatibility should exist among policies, instruments, and objectives. Unfortunately, that is often not the case. If the concern is income inequality, and the objective is to eliminate it, policies should be designed to close the income gap. However, labor policies are not very well suited to secure that objective. Education reforms are a much better instrument, albeit one with only a long-term impact. If the concern is unemployment, policies should have the objective of creating jobs not by the government providing jobs directly, except in emergency situations, but rather by fostering an environment for the creation of wealth, reducing as much as possible the transaction costs on labor-force adjustments of firms, and allowing each firm to offer employment packages that reflect its own specific circumstances. Consequently, labor policies can have a major impact on job creation. Securing flexible labor markets driven by market conditions induces wages to be set marginally below, rather than well above, market-clearing levels, which tends to increase economic activity, to affect profits favorably, and (usually) to increase savings rates. This, in turn, facilitates increased levels of investment, greater competitiveness in international markets, and faster rates of growth, output, employment, and, ultimately, earnings (World Bank 1993). Moreover, wage restraint encourages the use of more labor-intensive technology and further employment growth, as the cases of the United States and East Asian countries illustrate.

It is often argued, citing the U.S. case, that labor market flexibility leads to job insecurity and increased job precariousness. As has been shown, however, the evidence regarding job insecurity is not that conclusive, and the precariousness argument is misconstrued. What could be more precarious than the current job situation in many LAC countries, with large numbers of informal, underemployed, and unemployed workers? Those who do not have any benefits or social protection are indeed in a precarious situation. Consequently, policies that foster job creation based on reduction of labor costs and uncertainty about them, and that foster an environment for wealth creation and sustained growth, are the salient solution to the unemployment and wage stagnation problems plaguing LAC. While many of the jobs created in flexible labor markets, such as the U.S., appear to be mediocre, it is a better option than no or negative job growth, as in the segmented EU society, with the lucky few having high-paying, secure jobs at the expense of an increasing number of workers who are marginalized from the labor market with deteriorating or no skills, and with little opportunity to upgrade or acquire needed skills.

Regarding income distribution or wage differentials, it appears that flexible markets induce higher differentials, but the real story is about productivity and the increasing returns to more highly skilled workers. The problem is not that the differential is increasing—that is really to be expected and, arguably, applauded; wages send signals reflecting scarcity and productivity, providing incentives to acquire skills.[24] The problem is where, when, and why those signals might be ignored. This, fundamentally, is a problem of education and information and the workings of labor markets. In that regard the U.S. experience is likely to prove relevant to Latin America.

Main Public Policy Implications

• Temporary measures are often inadequate. When faced with increasing unemployment, the temptation for countries to resort to temporary employment-promotion measures is strong, but should be resisted. Given the long-term trends in labor supply and employment, and the scale and structure of unemployment, temporary interventions are likely to be inadequate, prohibitively costly, or even distortionary. While active labor programs and other temporary measures can be used as social safety nets and to build support for broader, more permanent reforms, they cannot be sustained for long periods. The often suggested policy options to help dislocated workers are (a) reverting—temporarily—to protectionism, which might help in the shorter term but would be counterproductive in the longer run since national income would fall, with its corresponding impact on employment, (b) better educating the work force, which is appropriate but is not a near-term solution, and (c) government-funded training. The benefits of the last option are uncertain and costs of universal training are prohibitive (the average cost of retraining per worker in OECD countries is US$7,000). While in LAC countries the costs would be lower, the total cost of training a significant number of unemployed would still be prohibitive. Clearly, government-funded training is not the solution to the unemployment and underemployment problem, and can only provide a partial remedy at best. While effective as an emergency measure, it often has no lasting effects. Such programs are at best an effective short-term, stop-gap option, with limited impact. Employment subsidies are an intervention that can be moderately effective. However, they run the risk of unproductive substitution of subsidized for unsubsidized workers. Evidence of the limited effect of these measures is shown in box 9.1, which describes the lessons from OECD countries. The encompassing OECD study concluded that remarkably little support exists for the hypothesis that government training schemes are effective. According to the study, the few successful occasions either have been small and focused, concentrating on helping people search for work, or have equipped workers with basic skills. Arguably, the closer the training is to general education (as in Germany), the more likely it is to succeed. But even then those programs are not, in themselves, going to solve the unemployment problem until the structural and institutional deficiencies of the labor market are addressed.

• Relying on growth will help mainly in the medium to longer term, and only under a regime of sustained high GDP growth rates. While the resumption of sustained growth will improve the employment outlook, it will do so only over the longer term. Given the scale of the problem, in most countries, relying on growth will not be enough to reduce short-term unemployment. With output elasticities of employment around the 0.2-to-0.4 range, the implication is that, all else remaining the same, to increase employment by 4 percent, a healthy 10 to 20 percent annual GDP growth would be needed. On the other hand, the wage elasticity of labor demand is usually much larger—between -0.4 and -0.8—meaning that a reduction of labor costs by 10 percent would increase employment by 5 to 8 percent.

Moreover, reforms that directly or indirectly lower labor costs are also likely to raise the output elasticity of employment and stimulate economic activity, so that their benefits are not "one shot" in nature.

Further permanent labor reforms are urgently needed. Authorities can influence market power in the labor market by modifying laws. Four groups of instruments can be distinguished: (a) union recognition procedures (the right to represent workers in collective bargaining and the obligation of employers to negotiate with unions); (b) statutory or administrative extension practices (that make collective agreements extend to third parties); (c) union security (the *ergo omnes* principle, for example); and (d) regulations concerning industrial disputes (for example, rights to strike and lockout, right to replace striking workers, and conflict-resolution mechanisms). The government can make a difference in labor demand and employment by making wage and employment-setting practices more flexible, reducing payroll taxes, and minimizing interventions that raise the minimum wage of workers.

• Since unemployment rates are highest for relatively disadvantaged groups, such as workers with lower education levels, these reforms may promote equity and income distribution as well or better than targeted interventions to help the disadvantaged. Certainly, labor market flexibility will lead to some job destruction, but that should be viewed for its positive effects; job destruction is usually a necessary antecedent to job creation. In the United States and other countries with robust em-

Box 9.1 Main Lessons on Active Labor Programs from OECD Experience

Since active labor programs are a common government intervention in periods of high unemployment, this box provides an overview of the OECD experience. Its main conclusion is that programs
have to be designed with a clear population target and measur-
able objectives. Furthermore, to become effective, programs have
to be continuously monitored, evaluated, and revised.[25]

Public works programs. Direct job creation programs are among the
most costly of active employment policies. In addition, experience
in OECD countries shows that they are among the least effective
in moving the unemployed back into employment. Although the
flow out of short-term unemployment may increase, long-term
unemployment is little affected. Examination of the postprogram
employment rates shows that the participants have a relatively
low probability of becoming employed. These programs can be
effective only as a temporary emergency measure.

Self-employment promotion. Self-employment assistance can be beneficial. However, experience has shown that well-designed self-
employment programs will attract at best about 5 percent of the
unemployed. Those who participate are likely to be primarily male,
better educated, and in their thirties. The programs tend not to
attract women. Program costs, excluding administration, are
equivalent in most cases to paying unemployment benefits. Lump-
sum benefits cost about 20 percent more per claimant than unemployment benefits, but the added cost appears to be offset by higher
overall employment rates and higher productivity where the self-
employed create more capital-intensive enterprises. This conclusion may not hold in countries where unemployment benefits are
relatively low or nonexistent, because program benefits will substantially exceed the unemployment benefits available. Questions
also exist about the value-added effect. Roughly one of every four

small businesses would have been started without program assistance. This is the so-called «deadweight effect» of these programs. An estimated one of every two businesses started will fail during the first year, though each business started will, on average, create 1.5 jobs.

Retraining for displaced workers. Retraining programs are generally no more effective than job search assistance in increasing either reemployment probabilities or earnings. Moreover, in the OECD experience, retraining programs for displaced workers appear to be two to four times more expensive than job search assistance. Combined with the previous finding, this implies that job search assistance may be more cost effective than retraining in assisting displaced workers get jobs.

Retraining for the long-term unemployed. Few programs result in gains in either reemployment probabilities or wages. Some evaluations indicate that these programs are more beneficial for specific groups, such as women. Where gains in reemployment are observed, longitudinal studies indicate dissipation of the effects of retraining within a couple of years after the program.

Implications. First, it is necessary to evaluate retraining (and other) public interventions using sound techniques. While the nonscientific evaluations of retraining programs may present a rosy picture, based on placement rates and other informal evidence, analytic evaluations are quite discouraging. Relying on nonscientific evaluations may lead countries to incorrect policy conclusions. Second, rigorous evaluations, while not necessarily allowing a complete social cost-benefit analysis, can be useful for policy-makers in allocating public expenditures on labor programs. Reviews of evaluations find, for example, that job search assistance measures—which cost less than retraining but appear equally effective—may be more cost effective in assisting displaced workers.

Source: Dar and Gill 1998.

ployment growth, sectors and industries that claim the highest rates of net new jobs created are generally those that have the highest rates of jobs destroyed. Similarly, nations with high rates of job creation also tend to have high rates of job destruction.[26] Given the employment–unemployment outlook in LAC, further labor reforms with permanent rather than temporary impact should not be postponed. These reforms fall into two main groups: those that make the labor market more flexible, and thus indirectly reduce labor costs, and those that directly reduce labor costs.[27] The following more specific recommendations represent both classes of reforms.

Specific Reform Agenda

• **Collective bargaining.** Modernize the wage-determination mechanisms through decentralization of collective bargaining to the firm level, and reduce the government role in determining workers' compensation. The general level of wages should be determined by the macroeconomic and international competitiveness conditions of the country. Wages with reference to specific industries, occupations, firms, and individual workers should be determined by the profitability of the sector or firm, by the effort and productivity of the workers, and by labor supply and local conditions.

Restrict government intervention in wage-determination mechanisms to setting of the minimum wage; eliminate compulsory indexation; sever direct government/union links to limit the union's use of their political influence in wage negotiations; and eliminate monopolies in wage-setting mechanisms. Removing the legally granted monopoly power over negotiations from the hands of sector unions and decentralizing collective bargaining to the firm level can have a significant effect on employment and wage flexibility. This is likely to result both in higher long-term employment growth and smaller cyclical swings in unemployment, and to have a positive fiscal impact, with an increase in employment. International experience on reform of collective bargaining is quite compelling. Chile, Colombia, New Zealand, and Peru saw employment growth of 3 to 4 percent annually as a consequence of labor reforms. The *OECD Jobs Study 1994* shows that private sector employment in countries with decentralized collective bargaining grew 30 percent more than in countries with centralized collective bargaining. Finally, simulation exercises on the effect of decentralization of collective bargaining indicate a 4 percent reduction in the unemployment rate.

Additional flexibility in contractual modes is warranted. Its positive impact on employment growth is illustrated by the OECD experience. Unless wage negotiations are opened to market forces through reform of the industrial relations system, unemployment will continue to be the mechanism that brings the labor market into equilibrium.

- **Contractual modes reforms.** Allowing for broader use of fixed-term, temporary, and part-time contracts, exempted from compensation obligations, should induce increases in job creation even after accounting for substitution effects. These types of contracts should at least be allowed for the most affected and economically vulnerable workers.

- **Payroll tax reductions.** A reduction in payroll taxes would raise labor demand and, all else remaining the same, lower unemployment. This would directly impact the relative cost of labor. Importantly, it will improve market efficiency by closing the gap between labor costs for employers and the benefits received by workers (the tax wedge) and the opportunity cost of time for workers. Given standard employment elasticities, a reduction of 10 percent in labor cost can increase employment by 5 percent. While payroll tax cuts are politically easier to implement than are collective bargaining reforms, they involve an adverse fiscal effect that may be considerable in the short term. The adverse fiscal effects of lower payroll taxes contrast with collective bargaining reforms, which actually would have a positive fiscal impact.

- **Severance payment system reform.** Severance pay is already an issue for short-term employment spells and, sooner or later, the impact of the severance formula will become a major labor market concern. Eliminating mandated severance benefits entirely, and replacing them with a fully funded severance payment system, should be considered. Since severance payment obligations impose an imputed tax of between 5 and 12 percent of wages, replacing this obligation with a capitalized fund for each individual worker, funded by an employer contribution of 3 to 4 percent of wages up to a maximum, would imply an employment increase of about 2 percent, given a common employment wage elasticity of - 0.5. Some Latin American countries with similar severance laws have already successfully transformed their severance payment systems into a deferred compensation scheme. Moreover, those types of funds are nondistortionary, since they do not create disincentives for job searching once an individual is unemployed, as opposed to the traditional unemployment insurance schemes that do create disincentives.

- **Workers' compensation insurance.** In a number of LAC countries there is no established workers' compensation insurance in the event of a labor-related accident. The consequence of such an absence is high imputed costs to the firm, mostly resulting from costly and uncertain litigation, with most of the expenses going to lawyers and experts. Quite often, small firms are the most affected, since a single suit can lead to bankruptcy. Adopting a modern workers' compensation insurance scheme can reduce those costs significantly and thus increase job creation. For example, in Argentina the imputed costs to firms before adoption of a national workers' compensation insurance system was 8 percent of the wage bill. After enactment of an insurance law, insurance premiums fell to 1.5 percent of the wage bill, on average, due to competition among providers and the elimination of litigation.

- **Data and information system reform.** Each LAC country needs to create a Bureau of Labor Statistics to systematically and periodically collect labor data. Current data on employment, unemployment, wages, and earnings are highly deficient, yet essential for policy analysis and design. A special emphasis must be placed on service sector data, given that area's major and growing contribution to employment. In addition, the current system of collecting, filing, and processing unemployment claims and listing vacancies is ineffective and inefficient. An accessible vacancies database should be developed, in cooperation with firms, for countries in the region.

Appendix 1
An Analysis of Informality for Mexico

In most countries in Latin America and the Caribbean, the informal sector constitutes an important share of both production and employment, as already discussed.[27] Moreover, this sector appears more active in terms of employment creation, although the quality of the newly generated jobs is a matter of debate. Therefore, it is crucial to better understand the nature of the informal sector and how it relates to the formal economy. In appendix 1, the results obtained by Maloney (1997) and Maloney and Cunningham (1997) for the Mexican case are summarized, in order to shed some light on the nature of the informal sector and, in particular, to understand what the relationship is between the formal and informal sectors (that is, whether they act as complements or as substitutes).

Two conflicting views are found in the literature on this subject. The first considers informal workers as the disadvantaged segment of a dualistic labor market, segmented by legislated or union-induced rigidities and high labor costs in the protected sector. This "decentralization" or "structural articulation" view argues that large enterprises, when confronted with increasing international competition due to globalization, use subcontracting as a way to reduce labor costs and gain flexibility. The formal and informal sectors are thus viewed as substitutes for each other. As pointed out previously, labor legislation in LAC countries can be described as very rigid and, most of the time, rather dated, especially after the sharp structural transformations that are taking place due to several economic reforms and increasing openness to trade. So, in principle, such a story might sound very sensible and appealing when trying to explain why the informal sector has grown so large.

The alternative view sees the lack of protection as one dimension of an unregulated but dynamic sector of small-scale entrepreneurs, most of whom enter the sector voluntarily, and who choose and are able to remain largely outside the regulatory structures. In this scenario, subcontracting relations with bigger firms could represent a *pareto* (efficiency)-improving change to avoid the inefficiencies in the regulatory framework, and need not imply a decline in worker welfare. In this case, the sectors would complement each other.

Using longitudinal data from Mexico for 1987 to 1993, Maloney and Cunningham tried to test for the validity of each of these two explanations. The dualistic view suggests that in the presence of above-market clearing and downwardly rigid formal sector wages, a shift in the formal sector labor demand leads to a rise in unemployment and increased demand for protected jobs. Displaced workers should find themselves looking for a job in the informal sector andthus driving wages down, relative to those of the formal sector. Trade reform, like that undertaken by most countries in the region, should increase competition for domestic industry, leading to a growth of subcontracting and a decrease in formal employment.

On the contrary, the "integrated" view suggests that workers contemplating self-employment will wait for an auspicious business climate before leaving a protected job to launch their enterprise: the size and transitions into the informal sector will be procyclical, and wage differentials should remain more or less constant. Greater international competition may lead to more subcontracting, but may not necessarily imply a decline in the welfare of workers.

During the period of the study, the Mexican economy went through a complete business cycle. First, 1986 and 1987 were years of deep recession and uncertainty about the success of the stabilization and reform programs. By the end of 1987, economic growth began a moderate recovery that would peak in 1990. While the recession seemed to have a depressive effect on wages, they grew in all sectors afterward as the labor market became tighter. Finally, the economy began to soften from 1992 to 1993, especially the manufacturing sector. Wages in the self-employed and contract sectors stopped growing and stagnated relative to formal sector wages, which continued to increase.

Two pieces of information are especially relevant for the analysis: wage differentials between the formal and the informal sectors, and the sectoral behavior of employment levels and worker transitions. Although some exceptions do exist, self-employment pays better than formal sector employment, and informal salaried workers systematically earn less than formal salaried workers. However, we need to be careful when considering evidence from wage differentials, because the assumption that a differential of zero represents an unsegmented market underlying many studies is probably unjustified.[29] Maloney and Cunningham's main conclusion is that evidence from wage differentials alone is not enough to discriminate between the two alternative views.

Contrary to the bulk of the literature on informality, it is the informal sector that is expanding as unemployment falls and growth picks up in Mexico, while formal sector employment decreases. Moreover, statistical correlations of intersectoral mobility and unemployment do not suggest that the primary function of the informal sector is to absorb displaced labor from the formal sector during downturns. Transitions into the informal sector decrease with rises in unemployment (considered as a cyclical indicator), although insignificantly, suggesting that—contrary to the safety-net hypothesis—it may be harder to get informal work during a recession.

Other authors have tried to explain this type of result (Revenga and Bentolila 1994), arguing that unemployment is essentially a luxury affordable only to those who are relatively better off.

On the one hand, the informal salaries show procyclical but statistically insignificant movements into formal salaried employment, consistent with the segmentation hypothesis; on the other hand, the higher the unemployment rate, the more the better-off members of the informal salaried sector enter the formal sector. There is no evidence of increased demand. This suggests a "safety-net" interpretation of informality for the lower tier, but an entrepreneurial view of the sector for the upper tier, where workers wait for better times to open their business or to join such businesses.

Taken together, these findings suggest that only a fraction of the informal sector exists because of segmentation, and that, consonant with other recent studies, the Mexican labor market is reasonably well integrated. The relative absence of rationing entering into the formal sector despite the very rigid labor code and high benefits may be due to the fact that the minimum wage is not really binding and, therefore, wages adjust in the formal sector to offset benefits and other non-wage costs, thus equalizing remuneration across sectors.

Finally, subcontracting appears to change in character across the period, arguably due to the opening of the economy. The great gains in contract wages across the recovery support the view that informality may arise partially as a *pareto*-improving response to the inefficiencies in the provision of medical benefits or pensions that make being paid in cash more desirable. However, the continued growth of the informal sector after 1991 at the expense of the formal sector, together with a fall in wages, would imply that subcontracting led to declining overall remuneration for workers—a decrease in worker welfare.

Further evidence comes from a study of a sample of small firms in Mexico (Maloney and Cunningham 1997), most of which are considered to belong to the informal sector. Maloney and Cunningham conclude that it is hard to justify the idea that the informal sector is primarily driven by labor market segmentation. After reviewing answers to questionnaires on reasons to work in the informal sector, such as capability and/or desirability of joining the formal sector again, age and education, and capital–labor ratio of the firms, we find some evidence that the sector does serve as a refuge for those unable to get salaried jobs, and this group earns somewhat less given its human capital. These facts would be consistent with this author's previous assertion about worse-off workers moving from informal sector jobs into formal sector jobs during economic booms. However, this group represents a minority of the population—roughly 20 percent—and to varying degrees it cuts across all age, education, capital–labor ratio, and earnings groups, making it difficult to point out some character-istics or common features that make the transition more difficult.

A large fraction of the firms are voluntarily in the sector, and are established or expanding. About 11 percent leave the sector, and they are often the youngest, but not necessarily those who entered the sec-tor because they could not find a salaried job. They correspond more closely to the failed, but voluntary, entrepreneurs who are usually found in small businesses. Besides, little evidence exists that the sector serves primarily as a way of reducing labor costs for large firms through sub-contracting, since only a very small number report bigger clients in-stead of individual customers.

In sum, it is difficult to conclude that one of the two explanations is totally correct. It seems rather that each characterization applies to a dif-ferent segment of the work force in the informal sector. It is very impor-tant to emphasize this point because economic policy and reform, and especially programs aimed at alleviating poverty, very often focus on the informal sector, looking for ways to bring all these firms under the um-brella of labor regulation. Undoubtedly a trade-off exists between protect-ing low-income workers and their families, and economic flexibility. Finally, we must keep in mind that the evidence presented here corresponds to the Mexican case that, similar as it might be to other economies in the area, possesses its own specific features.

Appendix 2
Evidence on Impact of Labor Market Rigidities, the Role of Unions, and Economic Performance

Authors	Goal of Paper	Main Findings and Recommendations
Bellman and Emmerich 1992	Review of empirical studies concerning the corporativism/flexibility/performance nexus.	Unions are bargaining for greater employment security for the already employed (insiders). Unions are ready to accept greater wage flexibility and even wage decreases, in return.
Blanchflower and Freeman 1993	Study of effects of Thatcher labor reform in Great Britain.	Reforms succeeded in their goal of weakening union power; may have marginally increased employment and wage responsiveness to market conditions, and may have increased self-employment. – Substantial improvement in the labor market position of women. – Reforms failed to improve the responsiveness of real wages to unemployment; they were associated with a slower transition from nonemployment to employment for men, and a devastating loss in full-time jobs for male workers, and produced substantial, seemingly noncompetitive increases in earnings inequality.
Blanchflower and Freeman 1990	Study of changes in unionization patterns in OECD countries.	American unions have greater effects on wages, but not on other outcomes, than unions in other countries. The high union wage premium in the United States contributed to the decline of U.S. union density and to consequent divergence of the U.S. industrial relations system from those in most OECD countries.

101

Buchele and Christiansen 1995	Study of possible effects of labor market deregulation in Europe.	Worker rights promote productivity and real wage growth (evidence is presented). Policymakers should be aware of these effects when thinking about reform.
Henley and Tsakalotos 1992	Study of effect of labor market institutions on economic performance.	The performance of highly centralized, or "corporatist," economies, such as Sweden and Austria, have in the past been superior to those of the EC members.
Milner and Nombela 1995	Study of the effect of Spanish unions on pay/employment flexibility, pay dispersion, and productivity growth.	Whereas unions are able to resist the pressure for widening wage dispersion, they are associated with somewhat poorer productivity performance.
Milner and Metcalf 1994	Study of links between Spanish industrial relations institutions and performance outcomes.	Evidence on the pay/productivity/jobs nexus and on the impact of minimum wage legislation on employment.
Heckman 1997	Study of the impact and design of labor regulations, particularly centralized collective bargaining, on job creation, and the effect of active programs	Evidence of the adverse impact on job creation of excessive job protection and severance payments and benefits, and centralized collective bargaining, and of the limited effect of active labor programs.
OECD 1996	Among other things, analyzes the impact of centralized collective bargaining on job creation.	Shows that net private job creation in countries with decentralized collective bargaining increased by 30 percent over a 15-year period, while it decreased by 1 percent in countries with centralized collective bargaining.

(Continues on the following page)

Authors	Goal of Paper	Main Findings and Recommendations
Cox-Edwards 1996	Through a simulation model analyzes the impact of decentralized collective bargaining in Argentina.	Shows that decentralization of collective bargaining would lower the unemployment rate by 4 percentage points.
Nickell 1997	Analyzes which features of labor market are responsible for the higher unemployment in Europe.	Shows that high unemployment is associated with generous unemployment benefits with little pressure to find a job, high unionization, and centralized collective bargaining, high taxes and minimum wages for young people, and poor educational standards.
Siebert 1997	Analyzes the impact of labor market rigidities on unemployment levels.	Shows the adverse impact on employment creation of institutional rigidities, centralized collective bargaining, high coverage rates, and generous benefits and protection.
Layard, Nickell, and Jackman 1991	Studies the impact of the coverage rate of collective bargaining.	Empirical analysis using cross-sectional analysis for 20 countries from 1983 to 1988 confirms that the unemployment rate rises with the number of workers or the proportion of workers covered by the collective bargaining agreement.

Notes

1. The main sources of the data quoted in this paper are World Bank studies, the International Labor Organization (ILO), the Comisión Económica para América Latina y el Caribe (CEPAL), the Organization for Economic Cooperation and Development (OECD) reports, and individual country household surveys.

2. For example, in Argentina the price of capital relative to labor fell by 40 percent during 1990–93.

3. For example, in Argentina the average annual employment growth during the 1980s was 1 percent, while the average annual GDP growth was –1 percent.

4. For example, in Colombia during 1991–95, the rate of real wage growth of skilled labor was almost four times higher than that of unskilled labor; in Peru it was three times higher; and in Mexico it was five times higher.

5. In countries with flexible labor markets (wages), the main effect of those demand shifts tends to be substantial declines in the relative wage of the unskilled (as has happened in the U.S.).

6. Technically, this means that the employment (labor demand) elasticity, with respect to economic growth, is larger for those countries with flexible labor markets than for those with rigid labor markets and that the effect is felt in a much shorter period (for evidence see OECD *Jobs Study 1994*). For example, in a rigid labor market context, increases in demand at the factory level are often met through increased overtime rather than through new hiring.

7. Unemployment recently fell to about 14 percent in 1997, mostly due to a combination of economic growth (8.4 percent in 1997) and a reduction of 10 percent in labor costs.

8. However, it should be noted that there are important, albeit indirect, linkages. Flexible labor markets facilitate increased economic activity and thus GDP growth, as has been argued in the East Asian countries (World Bank 1993).

9.   See Coe and Snower 1997 for an empirical analysis of the positively reinforcing employment effects of labor market regulation harmonization; or conversely the aggravation of existing distortions when job protection and wage and contract negotiations are liberalized on a piecemeal basis.

10.   For example, in Spain, 75 percent of employees are covered by collective agreements, although only 10 to 15 percent are union members. Similar patterns exist in LAC countries.

11.   In some countries, such as Argentina, the law allows that if a *"convenio"* lapses, the conditions established by it will be maintained until a new convenio is established. This is generally referred to as *"ultra-actividad convencional."* The effect of this type of normative structure depends on other aspects of the organization of the economy. For example, in the context of an inflationary environment, *ultra-actividad* encourages workers to go back to the negotiating table as soon as possible, while in an environment of general price stability, *ultra-actividad* discourages workers from doing so. To illustrate how binding the *ultra-actividad* clause is in Argentina, as of 1997, though 85 percent of collective bargaining agreements had lapsed, they had not been renegotiated but their clauses remained in effect as a result of the *ultra-actividad.*

12.   If *t* is the current labor tax level and *x* is the reduction in labor taxes, the decline on revenue in percentage terms will be given by *1-(1-x)(1+ 0.5t)*, incidence issues aside.

13.   See Kane 1992 for Brazil, and Bour 1995 for Argentina.

14.   Her model is based on the Mortensen and Pissarides (1994) job creation and job destruction model, which focuses on the frequency and duration of unemployment spells. The basic feature of the model is that wages are determined by voluntary agreements between employers and workers, and employment and unemployment decisions are made as a function of cost-benefit analysis. Prices and wages reflect relative scarcity in the economy, but in the labor market, bargaining power affects real wages, job search, and, thus, unemployment. Payroll taxes tend to increase labor costs and tend to reduce real wages, with a negative effect on employment. The effect on unemployment is a function of the parameters of the model, including the degree of bargaining power. The higher the level of workers' market power the higher the resulting wage, whatever the tightness of the market. The model simulates that, in the absence of a change in the industrial relations system, inflation control and trade opening result

in higher and longer-duration unemployment. These two necessary and successful policy changes (trade opening and inflation control) were followed by payroll tax reductions. Tax reductions generally result in higher net wages and lower labor costs, inducing more employment creation and also attracting more participants into the labor force. Given the level of initial unemployment in Argentina, tax reduction would be expected mainly to generate reductions in labor costs and additional employment creation. But in the absence of reform of the industrial relations system, the labor market may clear with a further increase in the unemployment rate (although with shorter unemployment durations). The effect of reform of the labor law that eliminates inertia in collective bargaining is simulated through a reduction in workers' bargaining power. The simulated impact is lower labor costs, higher employment, a negative effect on unemployment, and a reduction in unemployment duration.

15.   Based on Cortazar 1995.

16.   Based on World Bank 1997b.

17.   These attributes are region, urban/rural, gender, age, education, and occupation.

18.   Although this effect could be due to a higher rotation of workers in and out of a job.

19.   The data quoted in this section are from various OECD reports and the U.S. Bureau of Labor Statistics.

20.   As a consequence of those labor market restrictions, Spain has lost 510,000 jobs since 1990, 17.2 percent of total employment, in part due to the exodus of multinationals. Spain had no more jobs in 1994 than it had in 1964, even though population grew by 25 percent during that time.

21.   See also *The Economist* 1995.

22.   This should not in any way be construed as an indictment of all the ILO conventions or as a recommendation against their adoption. In fact, many of the conventions are quite desirable, with a significant positive welfare impact, and the East Asian countries would benefit from the adoption of additional ILO conventions. In addition, their impact on labor markets depends on how they are implemented. They are used here essentially as a proxy for the extent of labor market regulation and labor costs.

23.   Sectoral employment performance has also been found to depend on intraindustry wage dispersion. In Germany, for example, intraindustry wage dispersion and employment growth are linked through higher entry rates of new businesses, particularly small firms that can compete with incumbent firms through hiring lower-paid workers (Boeri 1990 and Hammermesh 1993).

24.   After all, if convenience store cashiering were as lucrative as, say, software troubleshooting, there would be little incentive for one to invest in the skills of the latter.

25.   The importance of understanding what should be and what are the aims behind government policy in job creation is illustrated in the following story: While touring China a Western businessman came upon a team of nearly 100 workers building an earthen dam with shovels. The businessman commented to a local official that with an earth-moving machine, a single worker could create the dam in an afternoon. The official's curious response was, "Yes, but think of all the *unemployment* that would create." "Oh", said the businessman, "I though you were building a dam. If it's *jobs* you want to create, then take away their shovels and give them spoons!" (Jordan 1996).

26.   In modern economies, job creation tends to be preceded by the destruction of some less efficient and, therefore, less prosperous jobs. The correlation between job creation and destruction rates by industry in the U.S. from 1973 to 1988 is 0.77 percent, as calculated from data in Davis, Haltiwanger, and Schuh 1996, table 3.1.

27.   Given the adverse short-term fiscal effects of further reductions in payroll tax rates, the latter are usually preferred.

28.   Evidence for this section is based on Maloney 1997 and Maloney and Cunningham 1997.

29.   This would be true if workers in both sectors were identical in terms of both observables and unobservables. Otherwise, wage differentials may very well represent compensating wage differentials. However, if the value of the unobservables remains constant over time, then a widening or narrowing of the wage differentials across the business cycle would be evidence in support of the dualistic view.

Bibliography

Agacino, Rafael. "Acumulación, Distribución y Consensos en Chile." *Revista Economía y Trabajo* 11:4 (1994).

Amadeo, E. J., J. M. Camargo, G. M. Gonzaga, E. Hernandez Laos, D. Martinez, A. Reyes, H. Szretter, and V. E. Tokman, (eds.), 1997. "Costos Laborales y Competitividad Industrial en América Latina." International Labor Organization, Geneva, Switzerland.

Anderson Schaffner, Julie. "Rural Labor Legislation and Permanent Agricultural Employment in Northeastern Brazil." *World Development* 21:5 (1993): 705–719.

Bellmann, L., and K. Emmerich. "Union Bargaining, Wage Differentials and Employment." *Labour* 6:2 (Autumn 1992)..

Blanchflower, D. G., and R. B. Freeman. 1990. "Going Different Ways: Unionism in the U.S. and Other Advanced OECD Countries." London School of Economics Center for Economic Performance Discussion Paper No. 5. London..

———. "Did the Thatcher Reforms Change British Labor Market Performance?" London School of Economics Center for Economic Performance Discussion Paper No. 168 (August 1993). London.

Boal, W. M., and M. R. Ransom. "Monopoly in the Labor Market." *Journal of Economic Literature* 25(March 1997).

Boeri, Tito. "Homogenization, Specialization, and the Sharing of Output Growth between Incumbents and Entrants." New York University Economic Research Reports (October 1990) :90–99.

Bour, Juan L. Mercado de Trabajo y Productividad en la Argentina. FIEL Discussion Paper. Buenos Aires (December 1995).

Bronstein, A. R. "Societal Change and Industrial Relations in Latin America: Trends and Prospects." *International Labor Review* 34:2 (1995).

Bruno, M., and J. Sachs. 1985. "Labor Markets and Comparative Macroeconomic Performance." *Economics of Worldwide Inflation*, Chapter 11: 119–134.

Buchele, R., and J. Christiansen. "Productivity, Real Wages and Worker Rights: A Cross-National Comparison." *Labour* 9:3 (Autumn 1995).

Calderon, F. 1993. "Pasado y Perspectivas del Sistema Sindical." *Revista de la CEPAL* 49 (April 1993).

Calmfors, L., and J. Driffill. "Bargaining Structure, Corporativism and Macroeconomic Performance." *Economic Policy* 6 (April 1988).

Card, D. "The Effect of Unions on the Structure of Wages: A Longitudinal Analysis." *Econometrica* 64: 4 (July 1996).

CEPAL (Comisión Económica para América Latina y el Caribe). *Estudio Económico de América Latina y el Caribe* (varios números).

Coe, David T., and Dennis J. Snower. 1997. "Policy Complementarities: The Case for Fundamental Labor Market Reform." International Monetary Fund Staff Papers 44 (1). Washington, D.C.

Cortazar, R. "The Evolution and Reform of Labor Markets in Chile." Presented at the Conferencia Sobre Mercados de Trabajo en America Latina. Buenos Aires, Argentina (July 1995).

Cox-Edwards, A. 1993. "Labor Market Legislation in Latin America and the Caribbean." Latin America and the Caribbean Technical Department, Regional Studies Report 31. World Bank: Washington, D.C.

———. 1995. "Labor and Economic Reforms in Latin America and the Caribbean." *Regional Perspectives on World Development Report 1995.* World Bank: Washington, D.C.

———. 1996. "The Unemployment Effect of Labor Market Interventions." Paper prepared for the Argentina Employment Study. World Bank draft. Washington, D.C.

Cuevas, A. 1985. "Sindicato y Poder en América Latina" (editorial). Alianza America. Monografias, Alianza.

Dar, Amit, and Indermit Gill. 1998. "Evaluations of Retraining Programs in OECD Countries: Lessons Learned." *World Bank Research Observer*. Washington, D.C.

Davis, Steven J., John C. Haltiwanger, and Scott Schuh. 1996. *Job Creation and Destruction.* MIT Press : Cambridge, Massachusetts:.

De la Garza, Enrique. 1997. "Trabajo de Investigación Derivada de la Encuesta: Contratación y Flexibilidad Laboral." Maestría en Sociología del Trabajo, Universidad Autónoma Metropolitana-Iztapalapa, México.

Diebold, F. X., D. Neumark, and D. Polsky. "Job Stability in the U.S." *Journal of Labor Economics* 15:2 (1997).

Reformas en el Mercado Laboral. "International News," *El País* (July 22, 1997)

Eurostat (Office of European Statistics and Communication). Brussels, Belgium. 1997.

Fallon, Peter, and R. E. B. Lucas. "The Impact of Changes in Job Security Regulations in India and Zimbabwe." *The World Bank Economic Review* 5 (1991): 395–413.

Fama, Eugene F. "Time, Salary and Incentive Payoffs in Labor Contracts." *Journal of Labor Economics* 9:1 (1991): 25–44.

Fields, Gary S. 1992. "Changing Labor Market Conditions and Economic Development in Hong Kong, Korea, Singapore and Taiwan." World Bank Policy Research Department Paper. Washington, D.C.

Freeman, R., and E. Lazear. "Longitudinal Analysis of Unions." *Journal of Labor Economics* 2:1 (1982).

———. 1995. "An Economic Analysis of Work Councils." In J. Rogers and W. Streeck, (eds.), *Work Councils: Consultation, Representation, Cooperation.* University of Chicago Press (for the National Bureau of Economic Research): Chicago.

Freeman, Richard. "Labor Markets and Institutions and Policies: Help or Hindrance to Economic Development?" Proceedings Volume of the World Bank Annual Conference on Development Economics (March 1992).Washington, D.C.

Godio, J. "Economía de Mercado, Estado Regulador y Sindicatos" (editorial). *Legasa* (June 1993).

Guasch, J. L., and A. Weiss. «Self-Selection in the Labor Market.» *American Economic Review* 71:3 (1981): 275–284.

Guasch, J. L., and A. Weiss. "An Equilibrium Analysis of Wage-Productivity Gaps." *Review of Economic Studies* 49:4 (1982): 158, 485–498.

Guasch, J. L., Indermit Gill, and Carola Pessino. 1996. "Estimating the Benefits of Labor Reform in Argentina." World Bank Discussion Paper 1371. Washington, D.C.

Guasch, J. L., and J. Monteagudo. 1996. "Structural Reform and Total Factor Productivity in Latin America and the Caribbean." Discussion Paper unnumbered. World Bank: Washington, D.C.

Haindl, Erik, Indermit Gill, and Claudio Sapelli. "Is Employment in Chile Becoming More Precarious? Evidence from a Labor Flows Model." World Bank draft (January 1997). Washington, D.C.

Hall, R., and D. M. Lilien. "Efficient Wage Bargaining Under Uncertain Supply and Demand." *American Economic Review* 69:5(1979).

Hamermesh, Daniel. 1993. *Labor Demand*. Princeton University Press: Princeton, New Jersey.

Heckman, James. 1997. "Diversity and Uniformity: Labor Market Reform in Argentina." University of Chicago Discussion Paper.

Heckman, James, Lance Lochner, Jeffrey Smith, and Christopher Taber. 1977. "The Effects of Government Policy on Human Capital Investment and Wage Inequality." University of Chicago Discussion Paper.

Henley, A., and E. Tsakalotos. "Corporativism and the European Labor Market after 1992." *British Journal of Industrial Relations* 30:4 (1992).

ILO (International Labor Organization). 1994. "Las Relaciones Laborales en Chile." Ministerio de Trabajo y Seguridad Social, Chile.

———. 1996. "Labor Overview: Latin America and the Caribbean." *ILO News*. Santiago, Chile.

———. 1997. "Labor Overview: Latin America and the Caribbean." Santiago, Chile.

———. 1998. "Labor Overview: Latin America and the Caribbean." Santiago, Chile.

IMF (International Monetary Fund). 1996. *International Financial Statistics Yearbook*. Washington, D.C.

Informe de Coyuntura Laboral del MTSS. Ministerio de Trabajo y Seguridad Social (December 1997). Buenos Aires, Argentina.

Inter-American Development Bank (IDB). 1993. *Economic and Social Progress in Latin America–1993 Report. Special Edition: Investing in Human Resources.* Distributed by The Johns Hopkins University Press for the IDB. Washington, D.C.

———. 1998. "Collective Labor Relations in Six Latin American Countries: Degrees of Autonomy and Decentralization in the Labor Regimes." Washington, D.C.

Jordan, Jerry. "Job Creation and Government Policy." Economic Commentary. Federal Reserve Bank of Cleveland (October 1, 1996).

Kane, Cheick. 1992. "Brazil: Fiscal Implications of the Social Security System." Country Operations Division, Country Department I, Latin America and the Caribbean Region. World Bank: Washington, D.C.

Kuttner, R. "The Limits of the Labor Market." *Challenge* (May—June 1997).

Layard, R., S. Nickell, and R. Jackman. 1991. *Unemployment: Macroeconomic Performance and the Labour Market*. Oxford University Press: Oxford, U.K.

Lazear, Edward P. 1990. "Job Security Provisions and Employment." *Quarterly Journal of Economics* 3 (1990): 699–726.

———. "Performance Pay and Productivity." National Bureau of Economic Research Working Paper 5672 (July 1996).

Leiva, Fernando I. "Flexible Labor Markets, Poverty and Social Disintegration in Chile, 1990–1994: The Limits of World Bank Policies." Unpublished manuscript based on Levia and Agacino 1994 (March 1996).

Leiva, Fernando I., and Rafael Agacino. 1994. *Mercado de Trabajo Flexible, Pobreza y Desintegración Social en Chile 1990–1994.* Universidad ARCIS: Santiago, Chile.

Lora, Eduardo, and Marta Luz Henao. "The Evolution and Reform of Labor Markets in Colombia." Paper presented at the Conference on Labor Markets in Latin America, Buenos Aires, Argentina (July 6–7, 1995).

Maloney, W. 1998. "Are Labor Markets in Developing Countries Dualistic?" World Bank Working Paper 1941. Washington, D.C.

———. 1998. "The Structure of Labor Markets in Developing Countries: Time Series on Competing Views." World Bank Working Paper 1940. Washington, D.C.

Maloney, W., and W. Cunningham. 1998. "Heterogeneity in Small Scale LDC Enterprises: The Mexican Case." Discussion Paper LAC Region. World Bank: Washington, D.C.

Marquez, G. 1994. *Regulación del Mercado de Trabajo en América Latina. Ediciones Iesa,* Centro Internacional para el Desarrollo Económico. Caracas, Venezuela.

Mazumdar, Dipak. "Labor Markets and Adjustment in Open Asian Economies: The Republic of Korea and Malaysia." *The World Bank Economic Review* 7 (1993): 349–80.

Milner, S. 1993. "Final-Offer Arbitration in the U.K.: Incidence, Processes and Outcomes." Research Series No. 7. Moorfoot, Sheffield (U.K.). Employment Department.

Milner, S., and D. Metcalf. 1994. "Spanish Pay-Setting Institutions and Performance Outcomes." Working Paper No. 9420. Bank of Spain, Madrid.

Milner, S., and G. Nombela. 1995. "Trade Union Strength, Organization and Impact in Spain." London School of Economics Center for Economic Performance Discussion Paper No. 258. London.

Mizala, A. "Labor Market Regulation in Chile: 1975–1995." Center for Applied Economics, Department of Industrial Engineering, University of Chile (May 1996).

Mortensen, Dale, and Christopher Pissarides. "Job Creation and Job Destruction in the Theory of Unemployment." *Review of Economic Studies* 61 (1994): 397–415.

Nickell, Stephen. "Wages and Unemployment: A General Framework." *The Journal of the Royal Economic Society* 92 (1982): 51–55.

———. "Unemployment and Labor Market Rigidities: Europe versus North America." Journal of Economic Perspectives 11:3 (1997.): 50–74.

1997 Economic Report of the President.: U.S. Government Printing Office: Washington, D.C.

OECD (Organization for Economic Cooperation and Development). 1994. *The OECD Jobs Study: Evidence and Explanations*. Parts I and II. Paris.

OECD. 1998. Employment Outlook. Paris.

Paarsch, Harry J., and Bruce S. Shearer. 1996. "Fixed Wages, Piece Rates and Intertemporal Productivity: A Study of Tree Planters in British Columbia." Mimeo.

Panagides, Alexis, and Harry Patrinos. 1994. "Union-Nonunion Wage Differentials in the Developing World: A Case Study of Mexico." World Bank Policy Research Working Paper 1269. Washington, D.C.

Psacharopoulos, George, S. Morley, A. Fiszbein, H. Lee, and B. Wood. 1997. "Poverty and Income Distribution in Latin America—The Story of the 1980s." World Bank Technical Paper 351. Washington, D.C.

Revenga, Ana L., and Samuel Bentolila. 1994. "What Affects the Employment Rate Intensity of Growth?" Working Paper 9517. Bank of Spain, Madrid.

Rogers, J., and W. Streeck. 1995. "The Study of Work Councils: Concepts and Problems." In J. Rogers and W. Streeck, (eds.), *Work Councils: Consultation, Representation, Cooperation*. University of Chicago Press (for the National Bureau of Economic Research): Chicago.

Saint Paul, Gille. "Labor Markets: How Reform Took Place." *Economic Policy* (October 1996).

Siebert, Horst. "Labor Rigidities: At the Root of Unemployment in Europe." *Journal of Economic Perspectives* 11:3(1997): 37–54.

Silverstone, Brian, and Bridget Daldy. "Recent Labour Market and Industrial Relations Experience in New Zealand." *Australian Economic Review* 104 (1993): 17–22.

Teitelboim, Berta. 1994. "Situación de la Pobreza en Chile: 1987–1992." Mimeo, versión preliminar. Santiago, May.

The Economist. London. (May 20, 1995). "A Chart Breaking Affair."

The Economist. London. (April 5, 1997). "The Politics of Unemployment."

Tokman, V., and D. Martinez. 1997. "Costo Laboral y Competitividad en el Sector Manufacturero de America Latina." E. Amadeo and others, Costos Laborales y Competitividad Industrial en America Latina. International Labor Organization, Geneva, Switzerland.

Turner, Dave, Pete Richardson, and Sylvie Rauffet. "The Role of Real and Nominal Rigidities in Macroeconomic Adjustment: A Comparative Study of the G3 Economies." *OECD Economic Studies* No. 21 (1993): 89–137. Paris.

Tyrvainen, T. «Real Wage Resistance and Unemployment: Multivariate Analysis of Cointegrating Relations in 10 OECD Countries.» *The OECD Jobs Study1994*. Paris.

U.S. Department of Labor, Bureau of Labor Statistics. 1996. *Monthly Labor Review* 119:9 (1996).

Van Reenen, J. "Employment and Technological Innovation: Evidence from U.K. Manufacturing Firms." *Journal of Labor Economics* 15:2(1997).

Westerhout, Ed W. M. T., and Jarig van Sinderen. 1994. "The Influence of Tax and Expenditure Policies on Economic Growth in the Netherlands: An Empirical Analysis." *De Economist* 142: 1(1994): 43–61.

World Bank. 1993. *The East Asian Miracle: Economic Growth and Public Policy*. Oxford University Press: New York.

———. 1995. "Workers in an Integrating World." World Development Report 1995. Oxford University Press: New York.

———. 1997a. "Estimating the Employment Benefits of Labor Market Reforms in Argentina." World Bank draft.

———. 1997b. "Chile: Poverty and Income Distribution in a High-Growth Economy." Report No. 16377 CH, April. Washington, D.C.

———. 1998. "Mexico: Enhancing Factor Productivity Growth." Report No. 17392-ME. Mexico Department, Latin American and the Caribbean Region. Washington, D.C.

Yamada Fukusaki, Gustavo. 1996. "Apuntes Sobre las Reformas Laborales en el Perú: 1990–95." Report #12. Centro de Investigación de la Universidad del Pacífico, Lima, Peru.